LECTURES ON SQL AND RELATIONAL DATABASE DESIGN

John W. Starner

ISBN:1480191825
ISBN-13:978-1480191822

DEDICATION

I dedicate this work to my family who have stood behind me always.

CONTENTS

ACKNOWLEDGMENTS

I would like to thank all of the students who have studied Database Management Systems in my courses over the years. Their kind and thoughtful feedback has greatly helped me in the development of this book.

1 RELATIONAL DATABASES

Introduction

A database management system (DBMS) is at the center of the data architecture of an enterprise. A DBMS provides a safe, secure, shared mechanism for one or more parties to work with the persistent information stored by an enterprise. This definition appears to be a bit vague, but rather than being vague, it is very wide and all encompassing. As the different parts of a DBMS are studied, the reader will begin to discover the true importance to the enterprise a DBMS is. The DBMS consists of data, hardware, software and people working together to support the operation of an enterprise. The DBMS provides a consistent interface for all of the users and application systems of the enterprise to access the data.

Functional Requirements

A DBMS must provide a safe, secure, accessible, shared environment to store the data of an enterprise. The DBMS must have a way of maintaining integrity of data that is consistent with the business rules of the enterprise. The DBMS must make the data accessible to technically savvy application developers as well as technically naïve analysts. The DBMS must provide for changing business environments and changing technical architectures. A DBMS must be:

Safe: The data stored in a DBMS must be protected from a variety of threats. There must be provisions to protect the data from incorrect values and usages of the data. There must be protection from system and network failures, and there must be protection from media and hardware failures. It is difficult to even imagine the loss to a business if data were lost or corrupted irrevocably due to equipment or systems failures. It will be one of the main tasks of a DBMS to provide a safe environment for data. The user and/or application system should not need to deal with or be responsible for the safety of the data. This will fall to the DBMS.

Secure: As data is shared across an enterprise, it is important to provide a mechanism to prevent inappropriate access to the data. It must be possible to provide and limit access to data at the "data element" level. It is important to control which fields of which records a user or application can access. Further it is important to control the type of access. Can the user view, update, delete, or create this data item. Providing the tools to implement this type of control is the responsibility of the DBMS.

Accessible: It is important that users and applications of different types be able to gain access to the data. It is also important in the modern interconnected enterprise that users and applications from different locations have access to the data in a seamless manner. This means that there must be in place interfaces necessary to provide this access. This is the responsibility of the DBMS.

Shared: It is important for more than one user to be able to access the data at one time. This must be done safely and correctly, however. Imagine the confusion of two family members accessing their joint ATM account at the same time. It is possible to imagine several scenarios where this joint access will provide incorrect results causing either the financial institution or the client to lose money. This cannot be allowed. The DBMS must provide a mechanism and protocol for application development that will always ensure the integrity of the data when multiple users are accessing the data.

The Database Management System

It is clear from the description of the task provided that a database management system includes software, hardware, persons and processes. The system integrates some form of permanent external storage media with systems application development tools and user access tools. At first glance a DBMS appears like a file system, though the requirements placed on the system are much more complex than a file system can support. Since the DBMS is to manage the persistent data of an enterprise, the DBMS must work with permanent external storage. It must do this in an efficient yet safe way.

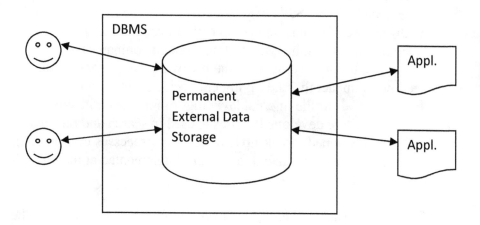

A database management system must keep data in such a way as to maintain the integrity if the business rules of the enterprise, and it must make this data available to users and applications within the context of a security schema, and it must store the data on external media. The applications and user reporting requirements are often developed independently of the design of the database and the DBMS system. The enterprise should be able to add or remove users and applications without needing to make adjustments to the design of the database. Further one must be able to make adjustments to the business rules and the database design without forcing the applications and user interfaces to change. The hardware requirements for storage of the data must also be separately defined. Finally it should be possible for the underlying hardware to be changed without the need to redesign the database, or the user applications and interfaces. For this reason the *Three-Tier Architecture* was developed. The three-tier architecture is so fundamental to the DBMS concept that it was developed as an ANSI (American National Standards Institute) Standard. In the Three Tier Architectures there are three distinct and separate layers.

Internal Layer: This is the layer at which the hardware is addressed. The mechanisms for writing and reading data from external media are defined and implemented at this layer. This layer is defined in such a way that changes in the hardware and hardware specifications are completely transparent to the other layers. This allows the DBMS development companies to be responsive to improvements in the hardware components without needing to impact the underlying enterprise business rules or use of the databases. At the internal layer algorithms for rapid storage and retrieval are developed. Indexes used in search and retrieval tools are developed. Back-up and recovery processes to protect the data from system and media failure are implemented at the internal layer.

Conceptual Layer: This is the layer that the enterprise view of the database is actualized. At this layer the entities of the enterprise about which data is to be stored are described, and the relationships between these entities are described. This is often done in a process entitled *entity-relationship modeling*. The entities are modeled in such a way that they are simple and contain no implicit business rules. This process is often called *normalization*. Finally, there are often restrictions on the values that can be used to describe an instance of an entity. *Integrity constraints* are

4

implemented at the conceptual layer. At the conceptual layer there is no concern for how the data will be stored, and there is no attention paid to how the data will be used in the applications. At this layer only the business entities their relationships and their constraints are defined.

External Layer: At the external layer the interface to the data that is used by users and applications is defined. This interface includes implementation of security and application specific redefinition and formatting of data. At this layer a specific application requirement is defined and produced.

It is important for each of these layers to function separately from each other. For example, one must be able to change the hardware to newer hardware without having to change all of the applications, or one must be able to redefine the way en enterprise views customer accounts without having to change all existing applications, and finally it must be possible to develop a new application without having to change the hardware or the way the enterprise defines the data. The fact that these three layers must work independently is called *data independence*.

Data Independence

Date[1] provides a very concise definition of data independence. "Data independence can be defined as the immunity of applications to change in physical representation and access technique". Date was specifically addressing physical independence, however it is easy to see that the term can be easily applied to the implementation of a DBMS that supports all three of the layers in the ANSI standard three layer architecture. That is, applications are also immune to changes in the way in which the data is viewed by the enterprise. There are, of course, other combinations. It must be possible to change an application system without requiring change in the hardware or without affecting the enterprise view of the data. As the reader progresses through the

---

[1] An Introduction to Database Systems, C. J. Data, Addison Wesley, 2000, pp20.

text it will become more apparent that data independence is not an advantage of using a DBMS, but more so the definition of a DBMS. The concept of data independence will be referred back to at several points in the text.

The DBA

The database is usually such an important part of the enterprise information architecture that there is a functional title for the responsible parties, the Database Administrator, (DBA). The description of the DBA varies among companies, however there are usually six functional responsibilities of the DBA.

1. **Define the internal schema.** The DBA is responsible for deciding what the hardware requirements are, and implementing the hardware. The DBA also decides what indexes are needed and generates those. There are many performance considerations to be made in the physical distribution of the physical datasets that comprise the database on the physical medium. The DBA must have a good understanding of the underlying operating system.

2. **Define the conceptual schema.** The DBA takes a leadership role in the entity relationship modeling process. While the nature of the entities is usually designed by functional personnel in the enterprise, the DBA provides the technical leadership and experience in modeling to correctly model the enterprise. This includes normalization and integrity constraint design.

3. **Define the external schema.** Different applications and different users will need to view the data in different ways. The DBA defines and implements the different user *views*. The DBA also provides user assistance and interfacing. As the reader will soon discover, retrieving data from a database can get quite complicated. Most users of a database are functional users and require some technical assistance.

4. **Define the security schema.** In any database environment it is important to limit the access that users have to only that which they need. A user should be able to access only those items they have need for. Further it is important to limit the type of access (read, write, create or delete). The development of a consistent schema for security, and the implementation of the schema are responsibilities of the DBA.

5. **Provide back-up and recovery.** Computers, computer hardware and computer systems are clearly not infallible. The data stored in a database often represent a valuable resource of the enterprise. It is essential that the enterprise be protected from all forms of loss. Losses can come from all types of situations from hardware failure, natural disaster, application failure, and other failures. The DBA must provide protection from all failures. The DBMS will provide an excellent toolkit for back-up and recovery that the DBA must effectively apply.

6. **Performance monitoring.** In an enterprise the DBMS is usually at the core of an application system that must be responsive to users. As the number of users, complexity of applications, volume of data and other factors change, the performance of a DBMS will change. It is important to monitor continuously the changes in performance, and take action that is needed to provide good performance. Most DBMS systems provide a good toolkit that will allow a DBA to anticipate performance issues.

Examples of DBMS

The following set of brief discussions of DBMS systems is not meant to be complete, nor is it meant as any form of endorsement for a product. There are many DBMS systems available. The criteria for inclusion of a DBMS in this list is the Author's experience.

Oracle

The Oracle© Company was founded in 1977, and in 2003 employs more than 42,000 and has revenues in excess of $10B. Oracle is the largest database company in the world. Oracle not only provides a DBMS system, but complete enterprise integration. Of the Fortune 100 companies, 98 use Oracle software in some form. In 2004, Oracle is marketing the ORACLE 11i database system and applications server.

http://www.oracle.com/

SQL Server

The Microsoft Corporation markets the SQL Server (pronounce sequel server) product. This product is a scalable enterprise database server system. It is designed to run in servers running Microsoft enterprise operating systems like Windows NT Server and Windows 2000 Advanced Server. It is designed in conjunction with the Microsoft .NET architecture for Internet based applications.

http://www.microsoft.com/sql/default.asp

IBM DB2

IBM's DB2 database software is the worldwide market share leader in the industry and marks the next stage in the evolution of the relational database. It is the industry's first multimedia, Web-ready relational database management system delivering leading capabilities in reliability, performance, and scalability with less skill and fewer resources. DB2 is built on open standards for ease of access and sharing of information and is the database of choice for customers and partners developing and deploying critical solutions. There are more than 60 million DB2 users from 400,000 companies worldwide relying on IBM DB2 Information Management technology.

http://www-3.ibm.com/software/data/db2/

Sybase

For nineteen years, Sybase has pioneered new ways to move data fluidly throughout the corporate infrastructure, regardless of the data type, the platform, the database, the application, or the vendor. This is **Information Liquidity** — transforming data into economic value. With Sybase, companies can attain maximum value from their data assets by getting the right information to the right people at the right time. Because "Everything Works Better When Everything Works Together™"

http://www.sybase.com/about_sybase

MS Access

Since its introduction in 1992, Microsoft Access has become one of the most versatile applications in the Office suite. This versatility is evidenced by the rich set of tools that even the most experienced database user can take advantage of, while offering the same level of simplicity as the other Office applications for first-time database users. Access version 2002 extends this versatility by giving developers and more experienced users new functionality, enabling them to access and analyze their important data as well as build powerful new database solutions. At the same time, Access now makes it easy for beginning users to discover and use more of the existing application.

http://www.microsoft.com/office/access/

MySQL

The rise of the independent Internet Service Provider and the small enterprise use of e-commerce has in turn given rise to the need for a new type of DBMS. In this environment an e-commerce application is developed as a web based application. There are a good number of application development tools for this environment. If the applications are to make use of DBMS technology, then the Web server that hosts the application is usually called on to be the DBMS server. Since this server is shared by many different applications operated by many different enterprises, it is not usually feasible for a single DBMS to be available. MySQL is designed as an open source highly efficient DBMS that provides all of the functionality needed. It is available for use without a license fee, and is easy to use.

2 SQL, STRUCTURED QUERY LANGUAGE

Introduction

The *SQL* (pronounced ess-cue-ell, or alternatively sequel) is a language or tool for manipulating relational databases. There exists a concise ISO standard for the language, though most marketed implementations have added considerably to the standard. Most of the additions are to provide additional functionality. In this text we will use only features that are found in the standard, so the examples and exercises should work in any implementation of *SQL*.

The original ISO *SQL* standard was adopted in 1986. It was subsequently updated with the addition of new features in 1992. This version was named *SQL2* (alternately called *SQL-92*). The standard was once again updated 1999 to *SQL3* (alternately called *SQL-99*) with new features. Since this is an elementary introduction to the principles of *SQL* The reader will not need to be concerned about the differences between the three versions. The reader who wishes to explore the features and capabilities of the SQL2 standard might wish to consult the excellent work by Date and Darwin[2]. For those readers who wish to further explore the

---

[2] Date, C. J. and Hugh Darwen, *A Guide to The SQL Standard, Third Edition,* Addison-Wesley Publishing Company, Inc. (1993).

features of SQL3, the enlightening book <u>SQL in a Nutshell</u> by Kline[3].

The SQL language began in an article by Dr. E. F. (Ted) Codd in 1970 in the Communications of the ACM, "A Relational Model of Data for Large Shared Data Banks"[4]. Codd wanted a simple a simple descriptive or declarative language that could be used to manipulate the tables or relations that would comprise a database. The original SQL language, while elegant, had some severe shortcomings. In order to be a practical tool for use in business and industry the many implementations have added many features.

There are two parts to the SQL language, a data definition language, (DDL), and a data manipulation language, (DML). The function of the data definition language is to allow the developer to create, modify and remove data tables that represent some real world entity for which data must be stored. The data manipulation language is to allow the developer to alter the contents of a table by inserting updating or deleting instances of the entity that the table references. The DML is also used to retrieve and summarize the data from the tables of rational combinations of the tables.

The basic element that SQL manipulates is relational tables. A table, as we have stated, is a set of column headers describing the attributes of an entity, and zero or more rows representing the instances of that entity. The SQL DML language is designed to extract information from tables or to combine the data in tables to create new tables. The result obtained from any DML statement is a table.

The SQL language is a descriptive language. When using a descriptive language the writer of a program or statement must describe what the results should look like. In the case of SQL, the writer of a query specifies what the attributes of the resulting table are, and what the properties of the instances or rows that will be

---

[3] Kevin Kline Daniel Kline, *SQL in a Nutshell,* O'Reilly Publishing, (2001)

[4] E. F. Codd, "A Relational Model of Data for Large Shared Data Banks" *Communications of the ACM*, Vol. 13, No. 6, June 1970, pp. 377-387.

included in the resulting table. The writer leaves the details of how these rows are extracted from the original tables entirely to the SQL processor. This is a radical departure from the way most programmers think. A programmer familiar with C++, Visual Basic, Java or COBOL is charged with prescribing the process by which the result is obtained as well as the form of the result. These languages are what is called prescriptive. The first hurdle in learning SQL will be to begin to think descriptively rather than prescriptively.

Before a discussion of SQL can begin, a sample database will be presented. This database will be used for all of the examples. While this database is very simple, it has sufficient complexity to demonstrate all of the features of SQL. This discussion of SQL will begin with a discussion of the some of the general rules that govern the structure and manner in which the SQL statements will be presented. This will be followed by a discussion of the DDL or data definition language. The DDL will show how to create and alter the tables that are stored. This will be followed by a discussion of the DML or data manipulation language. The DML discussion will actually have two parts. The largest part of the complexity and utility of the SQL language is involved in the query or *select* statement. This will be presented first. The *insert*, *update* and *delete* statements are all relatively simple once the *select* statement is understood.

In no case is this discussion to be considered complete. There are a great many topics that will not even be discussed, and other topics will be only mentioned cursorily. Further, all of the examples presented will be rather simple and academic. It is hoped that the reader will gain a working knowledge of the basic techniques through this material.

Sample Database

The database from which all of the examples will be drawn is a very simple set of tables that might be useful to store course registration information for a set of students, courses and teachers. This is by no means an example of a good database for managing registrations. It is much too simple. These tables and attributes were chosen because the reader will likely be familiar with the relationships that exist between the tables. The tables are *Students*, *Courses*, *Teachers*, and *Registrations*. The table *Students* contains one row for each student. The attributes of a student are student number (*sn*), name (*sname*), and major (*major*). The table *Courses* has one row for each course being offered the current term. The attributes are course number (*cn*), course name (*cname*), teacher (*tn*) and capacity (*cap*). The table *Teachers* has one row for each teacher. The attributes are teacher number (*tn*), teacher name (*tname*) and department (*dept*). Finally, the *Registration* table holds one row for each course that is registered for by a student. The attributes are student number (*sn*) and course number (*cn*). For all of the examples that follow the following sample contents for these tables are assumed.

Students

sn	sname	major
S1	Smith	MIS
S2	Doe	MGMT
S3	Lopez	MIS
S4	Chen	ECON
T5	Dupres	MGMT

Registrations

sn	cn
S1	C1
S1	C2
S1	C3
S1	C4
S1	C5
S2	C2
S2	C4
S3	C3
S4	C2
S4	C4
S5	C5

Courses

cn	cname	tn	cap
C1	Database	T2	20
C2	Micro	T1	30
C3	Macro	T1	30
C4	Management	T4	25
C5	Programming	T2	20

Teachers

tn	tname	dept
T1	Jones	ECON
T2	Garcia	MIS
T3	Brown	MIS
T4	Kelley	MGMT

It is important to note the use of case here. In all implementations of SQL, the use of case in data fields is important. The student *Smith* is different than the student *smith* and the student *SMITH*. On the other hand, the use of case in the table and attribute names is implementation dependant. Some implementations of SQL allow the user to mix case of attribute and table names and some require the case of attributes and table names to match the case used when the tables are defined. In order to limit confusion, all uses of table names and attributes in this text will match the case used when the table is defined.

One final note about the data values for the example database is in order. Very simple values have been chosen so that the SQL examples to be developed below can be as simple as possible. In a production database these data fields will contain more realistic data. For example, it is likely that the data values for student number will be a ten-digit number, and the names might actually be represented in two attributes, one for first name and one for last name.

SQL Language Rules

The *SQL* language is, like all other languages, described by a formal grammar. This will not be a discussion of the formal grammar. The purpose of this section is to help the reader to understand how to read and apply the formal grammar in the construction of *SQL* statements. The grammar will be presented by examples. It will be clear what the syntax of the statements are, and what the limitations are.

All *SQL* statements are free form with spaces, commas, parentheses or end-of-line separating all of the elements of a *SQL* statement. The following two *SQL* statements are equivalent:

SELECT sn, sname FROM Students WHERE major =
'MIS' OR major
='MGMT';

SELECT sn, sname
FROM Students
WHERE major='MIS' OR major = 'MGMT';

The second is clearly easier to read and understand. This formatting is used by most writers of SQL, and will be used in this text.

In *SQL*, a statement is a carefully constructed set of reserved words, identifiers, delimiters, operators and literal (constant) values. A reserved word is a character string (usually a string of letters) that has a special meaning to SQL. The programmer must refrain from using these words for any other purpose than that defined by SQL. There are many reserved words in SQL. A complete list of the reserved words for the SQL, SQL2 and SQL3 standards is available in Appendix I.

Identifiers or names are words chosen by the SQL user to reference a great many things. For the immediate future, it is sufficient to say that identifiers are used to name tables, views and the columns within the tables. There are some conventions used for naming these objects that will be discussed at a later point. The syntactical rule is that a name or identifier can have up to 128 letters, numbers and underscores, ("_"). The name must start with a letter. The case of the letters does not matter.

Initially, only two types of constant or literal data will be discussed. Numeric constants or numbers are strings of digits possibly containing a decimal point and possibly preceded by a sign ("+" or "-"). Very large (or very small) numbers can be approximated in scientific notation as a regular number followed by the character "E" and an integer exponent representing a power of 10. Some examples of valid numbers are:

1   123   1.2   1.234   .1   -123   +123   1E2   12E3   -123E4   123E-4

The limits on the size and precision of these numbers are implementation dependent.

Character string literal values are any collection of characters delimited by single quotes. The reader who is comfortable in other programming languages should make note here. SQL uses the single quote while many other languages use the double quote. If the single quote is to be a part of the string, then two adjacent single quotes are used. Some valid examples are:

'This is a string.'   'BIGLETTERS'   'don''t worry'

As mentioned before, the case of characters in string constants is important. The two strings 'Smith' and 'smith' are not equal.

In SQL it is possible to form arithmetic expressions using both constants and column names as variables. The arithmetic operators are +, -, *, /, as in many other programming languages. As the reader would expect, * and / bind before + and -. To alter the binding order the parentheses may be used. There is no operation for exponents.
One other operator is worth mention here. It is possible to create a new string as the concatenation of two strings. The operator for string concatenation is || .

It is possible to extract a sub-string from a character string. The value of the expression SUBSTRING('Smith' FROM 3 FOR 2) is the string 'it'. It is the sub-string of 'Smith' starting at the third character and is two characters long. One final string related operation is the TRIM operation. It can be used to trim leading, trailing or both blanks from a string. The expression TRIM(LEADING FROM '   Happy   ') is the string 'Happy   ', the expression TRIM(TRAILING FROM '   Happy   ') is the string '   Happy', and the expression TRIM(BOTH FROM '   Happy   ') is the string 'Happy'.

There are some conversion operations/functions that are very useful. Often it is desirable to convert a string entirely to upper case or to lower case. The functions UPPER and LOWER, respectively, do this. Finally, there is the CAST function for converting data type. Two examples of the use of CAST are to convert a number to a string and a string to a number. If the

column named *QTY* in a table was defined to be a string, yet contained values we knew to be numeric then the expression CAST(QTY, NUMBER)
would convert the string to a number for use in an arithmetic expression. Occasionally it is important to be able to convert a number to a string, for example to compare with a string. An example is CAST(123, CHARACTER). This would convert the number 123 to the string '123'.

The CASE operation is useful for categorizing or translating data values. Consider the following CASE expression:

```
CASE
   WHEN Courses.cap <= 15 THEN 'Seminar'
   WHEN Courses.cap <= 25  THEN 'Small'
   WHEN Courses.cap <= 35  THEN 'Normal'
   ELSE                              'Large'
END
```

The WHEN clauses in this expression are evaluated sequentially. For the first conditional WHEN clause that is evaluated to TRUE, the expression takes the value in the associated THEN clause. If no WHEN clause is TRUE, then the value in the ELSE clause is used.

Data Definition Language (DDL)

The data definition language is the rules by which tables and columns are created, altered and dropped in SQL. There are actually many more objects that can be created, altered and dropped in SQL. These are beyond the scope of this current discussion. The descriptive verbs, create, alter and drop are precisely the names of the commands to be used in SQL. SQL objects are created using the CREATE statement. Changing the properties of an existing SQL object is done with the ALTER statement. Removing an SQL object from a database is done using the DROP command. Even though the immediate discussion will be limited to SQL TABLEs and INDEXes, Some other objects are: USER, DATABASE, TABLESPACE, DOMAIN, VIEW, CLUSTER, ROLE, etc. The nature and use of all of these objects is important to a database administrator, but of no immediate importance to the present discussion. All of the following discussion will assume that a database exists, the reader is an authorized user of the database, and the reader is able to log-in, sign on, or gain access to the database.

Tables are created in the database with the CREATE TABLE statement. When creating a table the creator must minimally provide a name for the table, and the names and data types of the columns or attributes of the table. Further, as an attribute is specified, the creator may declare that the attribute should never be NULL. The concept of NULL values is complex, and will be discussed carefully later. An example of a CREATE TABLE statement is:

```
CREATE TABLE Students(
    sn    VARCHAR(5)   NOT NULL,
    sname    VARCHAR(15),
    major    VARCHAR(4));
```

The statement begins with the CREATE TABLE command followed by the table name, in this case *Students*. For reasons that will be explained later, table names will be plural nouns that describe the underlying entity that the rows of the table represent. Table names follow the naming rules described above. The table name is followed by a comma separated list of attribute descriptions enclosed in parenthesis. An attribute description is an attribute name, again following the naming rules, a data type and optionally the clause NOT NULL. The data type is one of:

CHARACTER(n) or CHAR(n)	fixed length character string
CHARACTER VARYING(n) or	
VARCHAR(n)	variable length character string
NUMERIC(p,q)	decimal number of p digits
	with q digits right of decimal
INTEGER or INT	full-word integer
SMALLINT	half-word integer
FLOAT	floating point

There are many other data types, and an especially rich set of time and date data types, however this small set of data types will be sufficient to allow a wide variety of examples. Finally, note that the SQL statement is terminated with a semicolon.

Definitions for the Courses table, the Registrations table and the Teachers tables follow.

```
CREATE TABLE Courses(
    cn   VARCHAR(5)   NOT NULL,
    cname   VARCHAR(15),
    tn   VARCHAR(5),
        cap  INT);

CREATE TABLE Teachers(
    tn   VARCHAR(5)   NOT NULL,
    tname   VARCHAR(15),
    dept VARCHAR(4));

CREATE TABLE Registrations(
    sn   VARCHAR(5)   NOT NULL,
    cn   VARCHAR(5)   NOT NULL);
```

When each of these statements has been entered, the database will hold four empty tables, *Students*, *Courses*, *Teachers* and *Registrations*.

Changes to a table can be made using the ALTER TABLE statement. To add the column age to the table *Students* the following SQL statement would be executed:

> ALTER TABLE Students(
>   ADD COLUMN age INT);

To remove the *age* column from the *Students* table, the following SQL statement would be executed:

> ALTER TABLE Students(
>   DROP COLUMN age);

To completely remove a table and all of its contents from a database the DROP TABLE statement is used. It is quite simple. For example to remove the *Students* table the following SQL is executed:

> DROP TABLE Students;

Domains

The domain is one of the tools in *SQL* that helps the DBMS to more closely model business rules. So far, the only data types allowed for columns are numeric types, string types, Boolean and date-time types. These are the natural types in that they all have direct correlation to the underling computer architecture. This is often a bit too general. Consider, for example, the following column declaration:

> day_of_week varchar(20),

This column would hold values like *Monday, Tuesday, MONDAY, Mon, and mon.* Since this column can hold strings up to twenty characters in length there is nothing to prevent this column from holding values like Domingo, Lunes, Martes, or like Lions, Tigers Bears, or misspellings like Monady, Teusday, … Except for the silly values that could be inserted, all of these other candidate values have information value in the context of day_of_week. They all convey the intent of the column. They fail, however, when it comes to making use of them in queries. Consider the example of the table *ORDERS* that has among its attributes *day_of_week*, and *total*. A query that would find the total of all sales for the first workday of the week would sum the *total* entries for all rows where the *day_of_week* value was '*Monday*'. Since *SQL* is merely comparing strings none of the rows containing *MONDAY, MON, Mon, mon, monday, Monady,* and *Lunes* would be included in the total. This is not good. One solution to this problem is to write the query to make sure that all of the legal variations of *Monday* are included. This is not a good solution in that it is not possible to guess all of the variations up front. A better solution is to develop a business rule that defines explicitly what the allowable values for *day_of_week* are, and then to restrict that column to only contain those values. This way, the values in the table are always consistent. Queries are easy to write and unambiguous. The problem of deciding what value to use for *Monday* is transferred to the data entry application. If a user attempts to enter an incorrect value, the attempt will be rejected by the DBMS. This is often managed in data entry applications by providing drop-down lists, and by providing functions edit and correct near guesses and shift case as desired.

This is implemented through the concept of a *DOMAIN*. A domain is a database object that defines explicitly a set of allowable values that will satisfy a business rule condition. The set of values is often a finite enumerated set of values like *day_of_week*. Once the *DOMAIN* has been defined, it can be used like a data type in the creation of tables. There are three different formats for the creation of a domain. These will be presented by example. Consider the example named *DOW* which defines the *DOMAIN* from which

23

values for *day_of_week* are drawn. *DOW* is defined as:

```
CREATE DOMAIN DOW AS
( 'SUN', 'MON', 'TUE', 'WED', 'THU', 'FRI', 'SAT');
```

Now the table *ORDERS* can be defined as:

```
CREATE TABLE ORDERS
(OrderID          VARCHAR(10),
day_of_week       DOW,
total             FLOAT);
```

In another example, in order to establish consistency across an enterprise a business rule that states that names must be truncated so that they fit in 15 characters could be specified. This can be handled by defining a *DOMAIN* called *NAMES*, and using the domain in table definitions. For example:

```
CREATE DOMAIN NAMES AS
(VARCHAR(15));
```

Now STUDENTS and TEACHERS can be defined as:

```
CREATE TABLE Students(
    sn   VARCHAR(5)   NOT NULL,
    sname   NAMES,
    major   VARCHAR(4));
```

and

```
CREATE TABLE Teachers(
    tn   VARCHAR(5)   NOT NULL,
    tname   NAMES,
    deptVARCHAR(4));
```

The *DOMAIN* can be used to establish a range or set of allowable values without actually specifying all of the values. This is accomplished through the *CHECK( )* clause. Consider the example where a business rule exists that capacities must be between 0 and 100. A *DOMAIN* called *CAPACITIES* can be created:

> CREATE DOMAIN Capacities AS INT
> CHECK(VALUE BETWEEN 0 AND 100);

Then the *Courses* table is defined:

> CREATE TABLE Courses(
> cn VARCHAR(5)   NOT NULL,
> cname VARCHAR(15),
> tn VARCHAR(5),
> cap   Capacities);

As rows are inserted or updated in *Courses* the values in *cap* are restricted to be between 0 and 100.

Finally, the *DOMAIN* concept provides an important feature for handling unknown values. A domain can specify a default value. The true importance of specified default values will become clear in the later chapter when *NULLs* are discussed. To create a *DOMAIN* that allows four character majors that has *None* as default, use the following:

> CREATE DOMAIN MAJORS AS
> (VARCHAR(4) DEFAULT('None'));

The business rule for an attribute defines the *DOMAIN*, which is then used to define all the columns in all tables that reference that attribute. The business rule is now shared across all tables in the database, and entries in tables will be consistent. This makes it possible to *JOIN* tables on common type attributes.

It is possible to change a *DOMAIN* definition after it has been implemented. This is done using the *ALTER DOMAIN* statement. This statement has *SET* and *DROP* clauses for adding and removing the constraints. A problem should immediately come to mind. What would happen if the *DOMAIN DOW* were changed to only contain the workdays. Any existing values of 'Sat' and 'Sun' in columns defined by *DOW* of existing tables would now be invalid. There are cases where this can be done, however the best rule of thumb is to not *ALTER* a *DOMAIN* after it has been implemented. Finally, if a *DOMAIN* is no longer required it may be removed with a *DROP DOMAIN* statement. The *DROP* statement has an option of *RESTRICT* (default) or *CASCADE*. If the *RESTRICT* option (or no option) is specified, and the *DOMAIN* in question is in use the *DROP* statement will be refused. If the *CASCADE* option is specified, the data type of any attributes that reference the *DOMAIN* will be converted to the underlying data type of the *DOMAIN*. For example:

Create the DOMAIN MAJORS:

```
CREATE DOMAIN MAJORS AS
( VARCHAR(4) DEFAULT('None'));
```

Now add a value constraint in addition to the default clause:

```
ALTER DOMAIN MAJORS
SET CONSTRAINT ('ACCT', 'MIS', 'ECON',
              'MGMT');
```

Now create a table using the DOMAIN:

```
CREATE TABLE Students(
    sn    VARCHAR(5)   NOT NULL,
    sname   VARCHAR(15),
    major   MAJORS);
```

Now DROP the DOMAIN MAJORS.

```
DROP DOMAIN MAJORS;
```

This operation will be refused. No action will be taken.

Now try the DROP with a CASCADE option.

DROP DOMAIN MAJORS CASCADE;

The *DOMAIN MAJORS* will cease to exist, and the data type of the *major* attribute of the *Students* table will become *VARCHAR(4)*.

Data Manipulation Language (DML)

The larger part of the SQL language is the data manipulation language. With the DML rows can be inserted into, deleted from, updated and selected from the table(s) in the database. This is done using the *INSERT INTO, DELETE FROM, UPDATE* and *SELECT* SQL statements.

Rows are inserted into tables using the *INSERT INTO* statement. To insert into the *Students* table the row containing the values 'S6', 'Turner', 'MIS', the following SQL statement is executed:

    INSERT INTO Students
    VALUES ('S6', 'Turner', 'MIS');

There are several things to note here. First, the values must be in the same order as the columns were defined when the table was created. Second, note the use of single quotes to delimit the string data values. Of course, if the data type for a column were numeric, the quotes would not be there for that value. Finally note that all data in single quotes is case sensitive. However that data is entered, it is stored. Subsequent queries will need to match case with the data entered. (There are some slick tricks to get around case sensitivity that will be discussed later.)

If for some row, a data value is missing or unknown, then a different format of the *INSERT INTO* statement is used. For example, to insert the row 'S6', 'Turner' where the major is unknown the following syntax is used:

        INSERT INTO Students
        (sn, sname)
        VALUES ('S6', 'Turner');

This would insert the row and place a NULL in the major column for the row.

The discussion of the *DELETE FROM* and *UPDATE SQL* statements will be deferred until after the discussion of the *SELECT* statement as they use much of the same syntax.

Single Table Queries

The select statement is used to construct a result table from one or more tables (or views). The *SELECT* statement syntax is a description of the rows and columns of the result table.   There are many parts to the select statement, and these parts will be presented one at a time through a series of examples.
For each of these examples a request for data from the database stated in English will be made. This will be followed by a SQL query that provides the requested results. For example:

Show all of the data in the Students table.

        SELECT *
        FROM Students;

The asterisk indicates that all of the columns are to be included in the result table and they are to be presented in the order they were defined.

The result would be:

sn	sname	major
S1	Smith	MIS
S2	Doe	MGMT
S3	Lopez	MIS
S4	Chen	ECON
S5	Dupres	MGMT

Note that the columns of the resulting table are labeled with the names from the *Students* table. To list the columns in a different order, they must be listed explicitly in the query.

Show the student name, major and student number for all of the students.

        SELECT sname, major, sn
        FROM Students;

The result is:

sname	major	sn
Smith	MIS	S1
Doe	MGMT	S2
Lopez	MIS	S3
Chen	ECON	S4
Dupres	MGMT	S5

It is often desirable to rename the columns in the resulting table. In this case the column name *major* is the same, except case, in the resulting table and in the *Students* table. In implementations of SQL that are not case sensitive, (e.g. MS Access), this causes confusion. It will be necessary to qualify the use of the column name with its source table. This is done by writing the table name then a 'dot' then the column name, in this case, *Students.major*. This will be important any time there may be confusion about which table in a query is the source for a column.

Show the student name, major and student ID number for all of the students.

> SELECT sname AS Name, Students.major AS Major,
> sn as ID
> FROM Students;

The result is:

Name	Major	ID
Smith	MIS	S1
Doe	MGMT	S2
Lopez	MIS	S3
Chen	ECON	S4
Dupres	MGMT	S5

Sometimes it is important to report only a part of the data in a table.

Show the names of the majors students have.

> SELECT major
> FROM Students;

The result is:

major
MIS
MGMT
MIS
ECON
MGMT

This is not a very satisfactory answer. It is the correct answer to the request: *For each student, show the major.* Without distinguishing information about the student such as *sn* or *sname* this information is useless. In this case what was wanted was a list of the different majors listed in the *Students* table.

Show the distinct names of the majors students have.

> SELECT DISTINCT major
> FROM Students;

The result is:

Note that the results are ordered alphabetically. This is merely a side effect of the method *SQL* uses to determine the unique *major* values.

Consider another type of problem. If it costs $2.35 to print a student manual for each student in a course, then what are the total costs for printing manuals for each class.

Show the class number and the 2.35 times the cap for each course.

> SELECT cn as Course, 2.35 * cap as Cost
> FROM Courses;

The result is:

Course	Cost
C1	47
C2	70.5
C3	70.5
C4	58.75
C5	47

Notice that the formatting of the results is not very satisfactory. While formatting is not the task of *SQL*, many implementations of *SQL* have a *FORMAT* function that can be used to impose a regular format on numeric results. That is not germane to these exercises so the results presented here may sometimes have crude formats.

Any arithmetic expression involving values in a row of a table and numeric constants can be performed. The arithmetic operators are +, -, *, and / with the usual meanings and operator hierarchy. Parentheses may be used to override operational hierarchy as in any programming language.

Most requests for data only want those rows in a table that satisfy some criteria. The *WHERE* clause is used to describe the selection criteria. For example, consider the request to report the students in 'MIS'.

Show the names and numbers of all students with 'MIS' for major.

        SELECT sn, sname
        FROM Students
        WHERE major = 'MIS';

The results are:

sn	sname
S1	Smith
S3	Lopez

The *WHERE* clause is any expression that evaluates to true or false that uses field values from a row of the table or constant values. These values may be compared in the customary way using the comparison operators, $<$, $>$, $<=$, $>=$, $<>$, and $=$. It is possible to construct complex comparisons with the NOT, AND, and OR Boolean operators. For example, $20 < cap < 30$ could be written as $20 < cap$ AND $cap < 30$. As in most programming environments, in expressions that involve both the AND and the OR operations, the AND operation is done before the OR operation. This order can be changed using parentheses.

Show the Courses with cap between 20 and 30 or taught by 'T2'.

```
SELECT cn, cname
FROM Courses
WHERE (20 < cap AND cap < 30)
    OR tn='T2';
```

The results are:

cn	cname
C1	Database
C4	Management
C5	Programming

The comparison operators work for string or text data as well as numeric data. When comparing strings it is important to match case. Further, strings are compared lexically in the same manner as words are ordered in the Dictionary. For example:

Adam < Adame < Adams

All of the upper case letters are less than any lower case letter, so:

Zebra < adam

It is important to note that some dialects of SQL may ignore case in string comparisons. While this is not part of the SQL standard some implementations see this as a convenience to information workers. MS Access is one notable dialect that ignores case in comparisons.

Another important comparison tool for text strings is the "wild card" comparison using substrings. This is often used in performing searches in text-oriented data. For example, to search for Courses about programming one might search for courses whose name matches 'prog*' where the * may represent any string of letters. In this case the * is a "wild card". The * may be placed at any place in the stem string, and, in fact, there may be any number of * in the stem string. Since the string containing a "wild card" is not exactly the same as a string in the database the = comparison operator cannot be used. The *LIKE* operation is used. Consider this example:

Show all students whose major begins with 'M'.

```
SELECT sn, sname
FROM Students
WHERE major LIKE 'M*';
```


The results are:

sn	sname
S1	Smith
S2	Doe
S3	Lopez
S5	Dupres

Sometimes it is desirable to summarize the contents of a table in some way. For example, How many 'MIS' majors are there?; or What is the average capacity of the courses?; or What is the largest course capacity? There are five summary operations that can be done, *MAX, MIN, SUM, AVG,* and *COUNT*. Their meanings are obvious. Consider these examples of the use of these summary operations.

What is the average course capacity?

> SELECT AVG(cap) as Average
> FROM Courses;

The results are

Average
25

What is the total capacity of the courses?

> SELECT SUM(cap) as Total
> FROM Courses;

The results are:

Total

The *COUNT* summary is a bit different. *COUNT* is used to count rows, not summarize a specific field. Therefore the argument of count is usually *. If an argument is specified for *COUNT*, then the result will be the number of rows selected that are not NULL for the specified field. IF * is used for the argument, then the result is the number of rows selected.

How many 'MIS' majors are there?

SELECT COUNT(*) as MIS
FROM Students
WHERE major = 'MIS';

The results are:

Note that these simple summary queries always return a simple one-by-one table with the result as the only entry. It takes a somewhat more complex query to put these results into a context.

In all of the queries presented so far, the results have been displayed in the order that *SQL* prefers. This is usually in alphabetic order on the key column. The basic guideline on ordering of rows in results is that if the user does not specify an order, then SQL is free to present the rows in *any* way. In order to control the order of presentation of rows the *ORDER BY* clause is used. The *ORDER BY* clause is always the last clause in a *SQL* query. The syntax for the *ORDER BY* clause is:

ORDER BY *<attribute 1>* [ASC|DESC]
<attribute 2> [ASC|DESC] ...

In this case *attribute 1* is the major sort key, and subsequent attributes are subsequent minor sort keys. For each key ASC or DESC is specified to state the sort order. IF ASC and DESC are omitted ASC is assumed. Consider this example:

Show all of the students in alphabetic order within major groups.

SELECT major, sname, sn
FROM Students
ORDER BY major, sname;

The results are:

major	sname	sn
ECON	Chen	S4
MGMT	Doe	S2
MGMT	Dupres	S5
MIS	Lopez	S3
MIS	Smith	S1

Sometimes it is important to be able to summarize groupings of rows in a table. For example one might ask, How many students are there for each major? This is done with the *GROUP BY* clause. In the *GROUP BY* clause an attribute or set of attributes is specified. The rows in the table are separated into groups by the distinct values of the attribute(s). At this point it is very important to note that the collection of things that can be reported in the *SELECT* clause is limited. As soon as the rows have been broken into groups it is only possible to *SELECT* the *GROUP BY* attribute, summaries, constant values or expressions using these three items. This is easy to understand if you remember that when a *GROUP BY* clause is included, the *SELECT* is reporting information about the groups, rather than the rows. Consider this example:

How many students have each major?

> SELECT major, count(*) as total
> FROM Students
> GROUP BY major;

The results are:

major	total
ECON	1
MGMT	2
MIS	2

How many students who are not S1 are registered for each course?

> SELECT cn, count(*) as total
> FROM Registrations
> WHERE sn <> 'S1'
> GROUP BY cn;

The results are:

cn	total
C2	2
C3	1
C4	2
C5	1

This query showed that it is possible to restrict which rows are used to place into groups before the summary is done. Remember that in this query only the attribute *cn*, summaries, constants and expressions involving these things can be reported.

Consider now the query that determines which majors have more than one student. This query requires that one retain a *group* based on a property of the group. The *WHERE* clause cannot be used for this. In this case the *HAVING* clause is used. The *HAVING* clause describes conditions for the groups that are retained and reported. Consider this query:

Show all majors that have more than one student.

>   SELECT major
>   FROM Students
>   GROUP BY major
>   HAVING COUNT(*) > 1;

The results are:

major
MGMT
MIS

All of the possible clauses for a query have been shown. They are always used in the following order.

>   SELECT ...
>   FROM ...
>   WHERE ...
>   GROUP BY ...
>   HAVING ...
>   ORDER BY ...

The following query demonstrates the order in which they are used.

Show all of the students who are not enrolled in 'C1' who are enrolled in only one class in alphabetic order.

```
SELECT sn
FROM Registrations
WHERE cn <> 'C1'
GROUP BY sn
HAVING COUNT(*) = 1
ORDER BY sn;
```

The results are:

sn
S3
S5

Join Queries

Often the data to be reported is in more than one table. For example, one might want to produce a list of student names and the courses they are registered for. It is clear that the *Students* table is needed to find the names, and the *Registrations* table is needed to determine which courses the students are registered for. On close inspection it is clear that these tow tables have a natural link, the *sn* column.

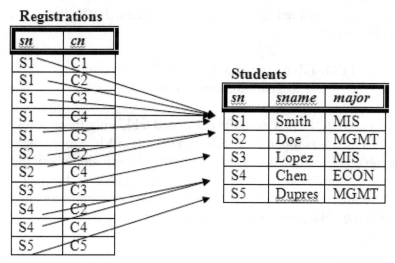

Registrations

sn	cn
S1	C1
S1	C2
S1	C3
S1	C4
S1	C5
S2	C2
S2	C4
S3	C3
S4	C2
S4	C4
S5	C5

Students

sn	sname	major
S1	Smith	MIS
S2	Doe	MGMT
S3	Lopez	MIS
S4	Chen	ECON
S5	Dupres	MGMT

For each of the registrations an associated student record exists. This is an important property of a well-designed database. This design feature will be discussed completely later. Because these tables share the *sn* column, they can be *joined* together on the common values in these columns. The joined table would resemble:

Registrations   **Students**

sn	cn	sn	sname	major
S1	C1	S1	Smith	MIS
S1	C2	S1	Smith	MIS
S1	C3	S1	Smith	MIS
S1	C4	S1	Smith	MIS
S1	C5	S1	Smith	MIS
S2	C2	S2	Doe	MGMT
S2	C4	S2	Doe	MGMT
S3	C3	S3	Lopez	MIS
S4	C2	S4	Chen	ECON
S4	C4	S4	Chen	ECON
S5	C5	S5	Dupres	MGMT

The *sname* and *cn* attributes can be selected from this combined table. This combined table is created through a *JOIN* clause in the *FROM* clause:

> FROM Registrations INNER JOIN Students
> ON Registrations.sn = Students.sn

The *INNER JOIN* places in the combined table only those rows where a match is found on the *JOIN* attribute. When more than one table is used in a query there is a risk of confusion about the source of the attributes. It is generally a good idea, and in fact often required, that the attributes be qualified by their associated table name. Here are some sample queries:

Show the student's name and class number for each registration.

> SELECT sname, cn
> FROM Registrations INNER JOIN Students
> ON Registrations.sn=Students.sn;

The results are:

sname	cn
Smith	C1
Smith	C2
Smith	C3
Smith	C4
Smith	C5
Doe	C2
Doe	C4
Lopez	C3
Chen	C2
Chen	C4
Dupres	C5

This combined table can be used in *GROUP BY* and *HAVING* clauses also.

Show the names of students with only one class registration.

> SELECT Students.sname
> FROM Registrations INNER JOIN Students
>   ON Registrations.sn=Students.sn
>   GROUP BY Students.sname
>   HAVING COUNT(*) = 1;

The results are:

sname
Dupres
Lopez

The combined table may be used with a *WHERE* clause also.

Show the students in 'C1' and 'C2'.

> SELECT DISTINCT Students.sname
> FROM Registrations INNER JOIN Students
>   ON Registrations.sn=Students.sn
> WHERE Registrations.cn='C1'
>   OR Registrations.cn='C2';

The results are:

sname
Chen
Doe
Smith

Note the use of *DISTINCT* here. It was needed because a student may be in both 'C1' and 'C2'. In such a case the student would be reported twice unless *DISTINCT* is specified.

It is not necessary to join on attributes that are keys. Notice that in this database *Students.major* and *Teachers.dept* are drawn from the same set of values. To determine all possible combination of students and advisors, one would *JOIN* the *Students* table and the *Teachers* table on the *major* and *dept* attributes respectively.

Show all student – advisor combinations sorted by student.

SELECT Students.sname, Teachers.tname
FROM Students INNER JOIN Teachers
ON Students.major = Teachers.dept
ORDER BY sname;

The results are:

sname	tname
Chen	Jones
Doe	Kelly
Dupres	Kelly
Lopez	Brown
Lopez	Garcia
Smith	Brown
Smith	Garcia

In fact, it is even possible to *JOIN* a table with a copy of itself.

Show all possible unique pairs of students in the same major.

SELECT First.sname, Second.sname
FROM Students First INNER JOIN Students Second
ON First.major = Second.major
WHERE First.snname < Second.sname;

The results are:

First.sname	Second.sname

First.sname	Second.sname
Lopez	Smith
Doe	Dupres

Notice that *Students* is used twice, once with an alias of *First*, and again with an alias of *Second*. The alias is established in the *FROM* clause. The name of the alias is separated from the table name by a simple space.

The *WHERE* clause in this query is needed to eliminate duplication. If the *WHERE* clause were eliminated the results would be:

First.sname	Second.sname
Lopez	Smith
Smith	Smith
Dupres	Doe
Doe	Doe
Lopez	Lopez
Smith	Lopez
Chen	Chen
Dupres	Dupres
Doe	Dupres

The *WHERE* clause First.sname < Second.sname eliminates the pairs where the names are the same, and where the second name is alphabetically before the first, thereby eliminating duplication of pairs.

It is possible to perform summaries on this combined table. Consider the query to determine the total capacity of all courses taught by each teacher.

Show the total cap for all courses taught by each teacher.

> SELECT Teachers.tname,
>   SUM(Courses.cap) as Capacity
> FROM Courses INNER JOIN Teachers
>   ON Courses.tn = Teachers.tn
> GROUP BY Teachers.tname;

The results are:

tname	Capacity
Garcia	40
Jones	60
Kelly	25

Since the combined table resulting from an *INNER JOIN* is itself a table, then it is reasonable to *INNER JOIN* that table with a third table. In order to determine the names of the students and the names of the courses they are registered for it is necessary to *INNER JOIN* Students with Registrations on *sn*, and then *INNER JOIN* that resulting table with Courses on *cn*. This would have the effect of associating with each registration the appropriate student record and then for these associations the appropriate course record would be associated. The *Students.sname* field and the *Courses.cname* field could then be selected.

Show the students name and the course name for each registration.

```
SELECT Students.sname, Courses.cname
FROM (Students INNER JOIN Registrations
      ON Students.sn=Registrations.sn)
      INNER JOIN Courses
      ON Registrations.cn=Courses.cn
ORDER BY Students.sname;
```

The results are:

sname	cname
Chen	Management
Chen	Micro
Doe	Management
Doe	Micro
Dupres	Programming
Lopez	Macro
Smith	Programming
Smith	Management
Smith	Macro
Smith	Micro
Smith	Database

There is no limit to the number of tables that can be joined in this way. For example if the Teachers table were subsequently *INNER JOINed* to the combined table in the previous example on

Teachers.tn=Courses.tn, then it would be possible to extract the teachers name for the course in the registration also.

For each registration, show the students name and the course name with the teachers name for the course.

> SELECT Students.sname, Courses.cname,
> Teachers.tname
> FROM ((Students INNER JOIN Registrations
>   ON Students.sn=Registrations.sn)
>   INNER JOIN Courses
>   ON Registrations.cn=Courses.cn)
>   INNER JOIN Teachers
>   ON Courses.tn=Teachers.tn
> ORDER BY Students.sname;

The results are:

sname	cname	tname
Chen	Management	Kelly
Chen	Micro	Jones
Doe	Management	Kelly
Doe	Micro	Jones
Dupres	Programming	Garcia
Lopez	Macro	Jones
Smith	Programming	Garcia
Smith	Management	Kelly
Smith	Macro	Jones
Smith	Micro	Jones
Smith	Database	Garcia

It is clear that the *INNER JOIN* is an extremely powerful tool for linking tables. It is a bit limited, however. Consider this query.

For each teacher, show the teachers name and the courses names that they teach.

        SELECT Teachers.tname, Courses.cname
        FROM Teachers INNER JOIN Courses
        ON Teachers.tn=Courses.tn;

The results are:

tname	cname
Garcia	Database
Jones	Micro
Jones	Macro
Kelly	Management
Garcia	Programming

On careful inspection of the data in the tables, it is clear that this is the wrong answer. One of the teachers is missing. The *INNER JOIN* by definition keeps only those rows from Teachers and Courses that match. Since there is no matching row in Courses for T3, Brown, MIS, Brown does not show in the result table. The query asked for all teachers. This will require the *LEFT JOIN*. The resulting combined table from a *LEFT JOIN* will contain *all* rows from the left table with their associated matches from the right table. Where there is no associated match, the fields are NULL. Using the *LEFT JOIN* this query is as follows:

For each teacher, show the teachers name and the courses names that they teach.

> SELECT Teachers.tname, Courses.cname
> FROM Teachers LEFT JOIN Courses
> ON Teachers.tn=Courses.tn;

The results are:

tname	cname
Jones	Macro
Jones	Micro
Garcia	Programming
Garcia	Database
Brown	
Kelly	Management

This is correct. The *RIGHT JOIN* works exactly the same. It keeps *all* rows from the right table, and those rows from the left table that match, substituting NULL where needed. The *OUTER JOIN* keeps all rows from *both* tables, substituting NULL where needed.

Nested Queries

Nested queries provide another powerful syntactical tool for writing queries. It is important to note that most queries that can be expressed as a nested query can also be written as a *JOIN* query. There are many queries that can be written as a *JOIN* query that cannot be written as a nested query and vice-versa. The nested query provides a different concept for constructing queries that is on some occasions easier to visualize in the development of complex queries. Nested queries provide the ability to, in a sense, develop a query top-down.

Consider this simple example. Find the course numbers for all of the courses taught by teachers in the 'MIS' department. This can easily be done with a *INNER JOIN* query. However, the nested query for this is as simple. It is:

> SELECT cn
> FROM Courses
> WHERE tn IN (*the set of teachers in the MIS*
department);

The phrase, "*the set of teachers in the MIS department* " is itself a simple query,

> SELECT tn
> FROM Teachers
> WHERE dept='MIS'

Putting these two simple queries together provides:

```
SELECT cn
FROM Courses
WHERE tn IN (SELECT tn
              FROM Teachers
              WHERE dept='MIS');
```

The results are:

Consider another example:

Who are the classmates of 'S2'?

```
SELECT sn
FROM Registrations
WHERE cn IN (the set of cn 'S2' is Registered for);
```

The nested query is:

```
SELECT cn
FROM Registrations
WHERE sn='S2'
```

combined:

```
SELECT DISTINCT sn
FROM Registrations
WHERE cn IN (SELECT cn
              FROM Registrations
              WHERE sn='S2');
```

The results are:

sn
S1
S2
S4

Note that *'S2'* appears in the answer set. Remember that this query provides a list of all of the students in the classes that *'S2'* is in. Clearly *'S2'* should be on that list. The *DISTINCT* is needed because a student could be in several classes that *'S1'* is in.

Queries can be nested arbitrarily deep. The development process is merely a step-wise top-down decomposition of the problem. Consider for example:

Show the Teachers names for the classes 'Smith' is taking.

> SELECT tname
> FROM Teachers
> WHERE tn IN (*the set of tn for courses that have
>   registrations by 'Smith'*);

the set of tn for courses that have registrations by 'Smith' is:

> SELECT tn
> FROM Registrations
> WHERE sn IN (*the set of sn for the sname 'Smith'*)

the set of sn for the sname 'Smith' is simply:

> SELECT sn
> FROM Students
> WHERE sname = 'Smith'

Combining the nested queries:

>SELECT tname
>FROM Teachers
>WHERE tn IN (SELECT tn
>   FROM Registrations
>   WHERE sn IN (SELECT sn
>   FROM Students
>   WHERE sname = 'Smith'));

The results are:

tname
Jones
Garcia
Brown
Kelly

Consider this important use of the nested query. The following query cannot be written as a JOIN query.

Which teacher(s) teach the largest class(es)?

>SELECT DISTINCT tn
>FROM Courses
>WHERE cap IN (*the set of maximum cap of courses*);

the set of maximum cap of courses is:

    SELECT max(cap)
    FROM Courses

Combining these queries:

    SELECT tn
    FROM Courses
    WHERE cap IN (SELECT max(cap)
            FROM Courses);

The results are:

tn
T1

In this case, the nested query produces a single value. In fact in any case that the inner query is a summary query it will produce a single value. In the cases that the inner query does produce a single value, the IN connector can be replaced by any comparison operator. The above query could be equivalently written:

    SELECT tn
    FROM Courses
    WHERE cap = (SELECT max(cap)
            FROM Courses);

Consider this query:

Find those students who are taking fewer courses than 'S2'.

> SELECT sn
> FROM Registrations
> GROUP BY sn
> HAVING COUNT(*) < (*the number of*
>   *registrations for 'S2'*)

the number of registrations for 'S2' is:

> SELECT COUNT(*)
> FROM Registrations
> WHERE sn='S2'

Combining these queries:

> SELECT sn
> FROM Registrations
> GROUP BY sn
> HAVING COUNT(*) < (SELECT COUNT(*)
>   FROM Registrations
>   WHERE sn='S2');

The results are:

sn
S3
S5

A nested summary query can be in the SELECT clause also. Consider this query:

For each student, show the sn and the number of sections Registered for by that student.

```
SELECT DISTINCT sn, (SELECT count(*)
                        FROM Registrations B
                        WHERE A.sn = B.sn)
                            as Sections
    FROM Registrations A;
```

The results are:

sn	Sections
S1	5
S2	2
S3	1
S4	2
S5	1

It is also possible to nest a query in the *SELECT* clause provided the query returns a single value. This can be a very useful tool.

Consider this query:

Find the names of the students and the number of courses they are registered for.

```
SELECT sname, (SELECT count(*)
                    FROM Registrations
                    WHERE Registrations.sn=
                        Students.sn) AS Courses
    FROM Students;
```

The results are:

sname	Courses
Smith	5
Doe	2
Lopez	1
Chen	2
Dupres	1

The Exists Query

The *EXISTS* format is a third way to design many multiple table queries. As with the *JOIN* and nested formats there are some queries that can only be done with the *EXISTS* format. After some simple examples to introduce the concept of *EXISTS* these special queries will be discussed. In an *EXISTS* query, a row of a result table is reported if there *exists* a row in another query result set that satisfies some condition relating the two rows. Consider this simple example.

Show the names of the students in course 'C1'.

```
SELECT sname
FROM Students
WHERE EXISTS (SELECT *
          FROM Registrations
          WHERE Students.sn = Registrations.sn
                AND Registrations.cn='C1');
```

The results are:

sname
Smith

In this case the *sname* is reported from a row in *Students* if there exists a row in *Registrations* that matches the *sn* for that row, and has *'C1'* as a *cn*. Another example is:

Show the sn for all students that are classmates for 'S2' in some class. Restated, find the students who are registered for a class for which there exists a registration by 'S2' of that class.

> SELECT DISTINCT sn
> FROM Registrations A
> WHERE EXISTS (SELECT *
>   FROM Registrations B
>   WHERE A.cn = B.cn
>   AND B.sn = 'S2');

The results are:

sn
S1
S2
S4

Note that *'S2'* is in the result set. If *'S2'* is in any classes, then of course, there exists a registration by *'S2'* for a class that *'S2'* is in.

Consider now the question, *For which Teacher has no classes?* To answer this consider the paraphrase, *Which Teacher does there not exist a Course with that Teacher?* This query uses the *NOT EXISTS*. The *NOT EXISTS* has several applications to answering queries that cannot be written any other way.

Which Teacher has no classes? Restated: For which Teacher does there not exist a Course with that Teacher?

```
SELECT tn
FROM Teachers
WHERE NOT EXISTS (SELECT *
        FROM Courses
        WHERE Teachers.tn=Courses.tn);
```

The results are:

tn
T3

This query determines which rows in *Teachers* do not have a row in *Courses* that match on *tn*.

The *NOT EXISTS* clause is used in another important type of query. Consider the question: *Which student is registered in courses taught by only 'T1'?* This can be restated as: *For which student registered does there not exist a registration by that student of a class that is not taught by 'T1'.* This peculiar use of the double negative logic provides precisely the result desired, and the double negative can be accomplished with a *NOT EXISTS* and a ◇ comparison.

Which student is registered in courses taught by only 'T1'?
Restated: For which student registered does there not exist a registration of a class that is not taught by 'T1'?

```
        SELECT sn
        FROM Registrations A
        WHERE NOT EXISTS( SELECT *
                FROM Registrations B INNER JOIN
Courses
                ON  B.cn = Courses.cn
                WHERE A.sn = B.sn
                AND Courses.tn ◇ 'T1');
```

The results are:

In addition to the queries using *"only"* queries using *"all"* can be written using the *NOT EXISTS* clause. Consider this question: *Find those students who are taking all courses.* This can be restated as: *Find those students for whom there does not exist a course for which there does not exist a registration for that course by that student.* This query uses the *NOT EXISTS* twice.

Find those students who are taking all courses. Restated: Find those students for whom there does not exist a course for which there does not exist a registration for that course by that student.

```
SELECT sn
FROM Students
WHERE NOT EXISTS( SELECT *
        FROM Courses
        WHERE NOT EXISTS( SELECT *
                FROM Registrations
                WHERE Students.sn=
                Registrations.sn
                AND Courses.cn=
                Registrations.cn));
```

The results are:

The Cartesian Product Query

The Cartesian Product is used by many SQL writers to generate an INNER JOIN. The Cartesian Product of two or more tables is simply the concatenation of all possible combinations of rows from the participating tables. The Cartesian product is indicated by a comma separated list of tables in the FROM clause. This is probably easiest understood through an example.

        SELECT *
        FROM Teachers, Courses;

The result is:

teachers.tn	tname	dept	cn	cname	courses.tn	cap
T1	Jones	ECON	C1	Database	T2	20
T2	Garcia	MIS	C1	Database	T2	20
T3	Brown	MIS	C1	Database	T2	20
T4	Kelly	MGMT	C1	Database	T2	20
T1	Jones	ECON	C2	Micro	T1	30
T2	Garcia	MIS	C2	Micro	T1	30
T3	Brown	MIS	C2	Micro	T1	30
T4	Kelly	MGMT	C2	Micro	T1	30
T1	Jones	ECON	C3	Macro	T1	30
T2	Garcia	MIS	C3	Macro	T1	30
T3	Brown	MIS	C3	Macro	T1	30
T4	Kelly	MGMT	C3	Macro	T1	30
T1	Jones	ECON	C4	Management	T4	25
T2	Garcia	MIS	C4	Management	T4	25
T3	Brown	MIS	C4	Management	T4	25
T4	Kelly	MGMT	C4	Management	T4	25
T1	Jones	ECON	C5	Programming	T2	20
T2	Garcia	MIS	C5	Programming	T2	20
T3	Brown	MIS	C5	Programming	T2	20
T4	Kelly	MGMT	C5	Programming	T2	20

On first inspection this looks like a large volume of useless information. If this product were to be restricted by only keeping the rows where Teachers.Tn = Courses.Tn by adding a where clause, the result is more interesting.

```
SELECT *
FROM Teachers, Courses
        WHERE Teachers.Tn = Courses.Tn;
```
The result is:

teachers.tn	tname	dept	cn	cname	courses.tn	cap
T2	Garcia	MIS	C1	Database	T2	20
T1	Jones	ECON	C2	Micro	T1	30
T1	Jones	ECON	C3	Macro	T1	30
T4	Kelly	MGMT	C4	Management	T4	25
T2	Garcia	MIS	C5	Programming	T2	20

With the exception that the Courses.tn column duplicates the Teachers.Tn column this result is the same as the INNER JOIN on Teachers.Tn=Courses.Tn . The clause Teachers.Tn=Courses.Tn is typically called the JOIN clause. This is the way that *INNER JOINs* are formed. In many dialects of SQL that have not implemented the *INNER JOIN* syntax, this is the way an *INNER JOIN* is produced.

There are other types of queries that can only be addressed with the Cartesian Product. These queries typically involve pairings of rows from the same table. Consider the reasonable request:

Find all possible MIS study groups, that is, pairs of students in the same major.

To do this a Cartesian Product is formed between two copies of STUDENTS aliased to *A* and *B* respectively. Then only the rows where *A.Major* and *B.Major* are *'MIS'*.

```
SELECT A.Sname, B.Sname
```

FROM Students A, Students B
WHERE A.Major = 'MIS' and B.Major = 'MIS';
The result is:

A.Sname	B.Sname
Smith	Smith
Lopez	Smith
Smith	Lopez
Lopez	Lopez

This result is less than satisfactory in that neither Smith, Smith nor Lopez,Lopez are valid pairs. Further, if Lopez, Smith is kept, then Smith, Lopez should be rejected since it represents the same pair. This can be handled nicely through a simple addition to the WHERE clause, AND A.Sname < B.Sname. This clause indicates that the row is not kept if the names are the same, and of the two rows that represent the same pair, only the one where the first name is less than the second name is kept. The modified query is:

SELECT A.Sname, B.Sname
FROM Students A, Students B
WHERE A.Major = 'MIS' and B.Major = 'MIS'
                    AND A.Sname < B.Sname;
The result is, as expected:

A.Sname	B.Sname
Lopez	Smith

The Union Query

The *UNION* query is simply the joining together in a single set of rows the results of two or more queries. In order for the resulting rows of two queries to be placed in a single result collection they must be similar. The two queries in the *UNION* must have the same number of columns with the same data types, in the same order. Two queries that satisfy this criteria are called union compatible. An example of a situation that would use a *UNION* query would be:

Find the names of the students in the largest classes, and in the smallest classes in the same table. Indicate in a second column whether largest or smallest.

The SQL is:

```
          SELECT Sname, 'Largest' AS EXTREME
          FROM Students
          WHERE Sn IN (
                    SELECT Sn
                    FROM Registrations
                    WHERE Cn IN (
                              SELECT Cn
                              FROM Courses
                              WHERE CAP = (
                                        SELECT MAX(CAP)
                                        FROM Courses)))
     UNION

          SELECT Sname, 'Smallest' AS EXTREME
          FROM Students
          WHERE Sn IN (
                    SELECT Sn
                    FROM Registrations
                    WHERE Cn IN (
                              SELECT Cn
                              FROM Courses
                              WHERE CAP = (
                                        SELECT MIN(CAP)
                                        FROM Courses)))
```

The result is:

Sname	EXTREME
Chen	Largest
Doe	Largest
Dupres	Smallest
Lopez	Largest
Smith	Largest
Smith	Smallest

INSERT, DELETE and UPDATE

The *INSERT* statement is used to put new rows into a table. Earlier the simple syntax to insert rows into a table was presented.

Insert the row 'S6', 'Turner', 'MIS' into the Students table.

> INSERT INTO Students
> VALUES ('S6', 'Turner', 'MIS');

It is important to note that if a row to be inserted will cause a duplicate primary key, the insertion will be blocked. An error message will be provided to the user. In order to use this format of the *INSERT INTO* statement, the order in which the columns were defined must be known.

If the order of the columns is unknown, or if for some column, a data value is missing or unknown, then a different format of the *INSERT INTO* statement is used. For example:

Insert the row 'S6', 'Turner' where the major is unknown.

> INSERT INTO Students
> (sn, sname)
> VALUES ('S6', 'Turner');

In this case the column names are provided to describe which columns the data values will be placed in, and which order the data values are listed.

It is also possible to insert one or more rows that are the result of a query into a table. In this case, a query is formed to produce the data for the row.

Insert a rows in Registrations for all MGMT majors that are not currently enrolled in Course 'C4'.

The query to produce the rows is:

```
SELECT sn, 'C4' AS cn
FROM Students
WHERE major = 'MGMT'
    AND NOT EXISTS( SELECT *
                FROM Registrations
                WHERE Students.sn = Registrations.sn
                7.          AND
                Registrations.cn = 'C4');
```

The results of this query are:

sn	cn
S5	C4

The student 'S5' is a 'MGMT' major who is not currently registered for 'C4'. To insert this row the following syntax is used:

```
INSERT INTO Registrations (sn, cn)
SELECT sn, 'C4' AS cn
FROM Students
```

WHERE major = 'MGMT'
      AND NOT EXISTS(SELECT *
            FROM Registrations
            WHERE Students.sn = Registrations.sn
                  AND Registrations.cn =
                        'C4');

The results of this query are to insert the row 'S5', 'C4' into Registrations.

The *UPDATE* statement is used to change values in a table. The *UPDATE* statement that would change all of 'T2's teaching assignments to 'T3' is:

Change all occurrences of 'T2' in Courses to 'T3'.

      UPDATE Courses
      SET tn='T3'
      WHERE tn = 'T2';
The result would be to change all occurrences of 'T2' to 'T3' in the Courses table. Consider this slightly more complex example:

Add 5 to the cap for all courses taught by MIS faculty:

      UPDATE Courses
      SET cap=cap + 5
      WHERE tn IN (SELECT tn
            FROM Teachers
            WHERE dept = 'MIS');

The result would be to change the cap on Courses 'C1' and 'C5'.

The *DELETE* statement completely removes rows from a table. Consider this example:

Remove all registrations in course 'C5'.

> DELETE
> FROM Registrations
> WHERE cn = 'C5';

This would remove two rows from Registrations. A note of caution is in order here. If you accidentally type and execute:

> DELETE
> FROM Registrations;

All rows in Registrations will be removed! In an implementation that *COMMIT*s each transaction like MS Access, all the data is unrecoverably lost.

3 VIEWS

Introduction

The view database object is a very powerful tool. It is the tool that provides the data independence link between the conceptual layer and the external layer of the ANSI three-layer standard. A view is a virtual table. To an *SQL* query a view appears exactly like a base table. A view has no data associated with it. It is merely a mapping of base tables and other views to form a table. A user looks at the data in the base tables through the mapping. This provides the ability to alter the conceptual view of the database, that is, restructure the base tables, without affecting the end users or application programs. When the DBA makes a change to the base tables due to changes in the enterprise view of the entities and relationships, appropriate changes are made to the views that the users and application programs use so that they continue to perceive the underlying data in the same way.

Views also provide a mechanism for providing data field level security. It is possible to construct a view so that only certain rows and columns of the base tables are visible. The user is granted access to only the needed views, and the desired security is achieved. This will be demonstrated through some simple examples.

Finally, views provide a mechanism to simplify writing queries. Many end-users are not sufficiently sophisticated in competency with *SQL* to construct *JOIN*s, nested queries, *GROUP BY* queries, *EXISTS* queries, etc. Yet the result sets they wish require these constructs. The DBA can construct views that embody the more complex *SQL* features, and the end-user is left to select only those rows and columns from the view that are desired in the result set. This is an easy task. This also will be demonstrated through examples.

The View

A view is simply a stored query. The view has a name that is used as if it were a base table by end-users. Not every query can be made into a useful view. The set of rules governing the types of *SQL* will be presented later. The column names of the view are derived from the underlying tables unless they are explicitly provided in the query that defines the view. It is important to explicitly define column names where the resulting column is an expression, or where there might be ambiguity among column names. Consider this simple example of the view *MISMAJORS*.

```
CREATE VIEW MISMAJORS AS
SELECT sn, sname
FROM Students
WHERE major = 'MIS';
```

This will create the *MISMAJORS* view database object. No data is stored. The data that is viewed through the *MISMAJORS* view is the data in the *Students* base table. This view can be used in a query as if it were a table.

Show the 'MIS' majors:

```
SELECT *
```

FROM MISMAJORS;

The results are:

sn	sname
S1	Smith
S3	Lopez

Show the classes registered for by the MIS majors.

SELECT Registrations.sn, Registrations.cn
FROM MISMAJORS INNER JOIN Registrations
ON Registrations.sn = MISMAJORS.sn;

The results are:

sn	cn
S1	C1
S1	C2
S1	C3
S1	C4
S1	C5
S3	C3

It is clear from these examples how views can be used to make the queries end-users write simpler. Using the *MISMAJORS* view the end-user does not need to include the *WHERE* clause *major =* *'MIS'*. It is also clear how views can be used to implement data element level security protection. In the case of the view *MISMAJORS* a user would only be able to view rows where the *major* is *'MIS'*, and the *sn* and *sname* columns. The user has access to only some rows and some columns of the data table. In this way field level security is provided.

View Updatability

Since a view is merely a filter through a base table is viewed, it is reasonable to ask that the user be able to perform update operations on a view. Consider for example,

Change the name of all MISMAJORS whose name is 'Smith' to 'Smythe'.

> UPDATE MISMAJORS
> SET snamne='Smythe'
> WHERE sname = 'Smith';

This would have the desired effect of changing the name *Smith* in Student *S1* to *Smythe*.

Consider now the update to add a new MIS major:

Add S6, Turner as an MIS major.

> INSERT INTO MISMAJORS
> VALUES('S6','Turner');

The result would make the base table *Students* look like:

sn	sname	major
S1	Smith	MIS
S2	Doe	MGMT
S3	Lopez	MIS
S4	Chen	ECON
S5	Dupres	MGMT
S6	Turner	

Note that there is no major specified for S6. Therefore, the query

      SELECT *
      FROM MISMAJORS

Would produce:

sn	sname
S1	Smith
S3	Lopez

    This is clearly not the desired result! This happens because the user of the MISMAJORS query cannot access the *major* field to set the appropriate value. The value of the *major* field of the inserted row is the default value for the field, or NULL if no default is specified.

4 NULLS

Nulls in SQL

The concept of *Null* is an extremely useful and often poorly used one in SQL. *Null* is a typeless and valueless item. It is placed in a field value in a row in the database when a value is not supplied. There are several reasons *Null* might be required. It might be that at the time a row is inserted into a table (a) value(s) for one or more of the columns might be unknown. The(se) value(s) would be replaced by *Null*. Despite the difficulties to be described concerning *Nulls* this might be preferable to supplying some universal constant such as *0* or *–999* or *Unknown*. Further it might be the case that no value exists for this field for this row. Consider the field *FirstName* for a table containing name information. For some rows there may not exist a value for this field. (There are several popular figures who are known by a single name, Cher, Prince, Spencer, etc.) Finally it may be that for this field a value would be inappropriate for some rows. Consider the field *Spouse*. If the *MatitalStatus* field in a row is *Single*, then a value in *Spouse* would be inappropriate.

Problems With Nulls

Since *Null* is typeless it can be placed in any field in any column of any table. Later it will be shown that there are circumstances where *Null* cannot be tolerated in a column, and then it will be shown how to prevent *Null* from being placed in a column. Also, *Null* is valueless, therefore no value can successfully be compared with a *Null* value. If *A* contains *Null*, then the expressions:

$$A = B$$
$$A \mathrel{!=} B$$
$$A < B$$
$$A > B$$
$$A = \text{Null}$$

all have the value *Null* rather than the expected *TRUE* or *FALSE*, regardless of the value in B. Because it is useful to determine if a field contains *Null* there is an operation that returns true of false depending on whether the field value is *Null*. To determine if the field *A* contains *Null* the *IS Null* operation is used. For example, to determine the names of the *students* who have not declared a *major*, one might use the following query:

```
SELECT same
FROM Students
WHERE major is Null;
```

Conversely, to determine those *students* who have declared a *major*, one would use this query:

```
SELECT same
FROM Students
WHERE major is not Null;
```

Since a relational expression can now return three values, *True, False, and Null* traditional logic can get a bit confusing. There are now three logical values. This can lead to some surprising results. For the following discussion assume that the *Students* table can accept *Null* values in the *majors* column. A *Null* value would indicate that the student has not yet chosen a major. Consider the following version of the table:

Students

sn	sname	major
S1	Smith	MIS
S2	Doe	MGMT
S3	Lopez	Null
S4	Chen	ECON
S5	Dupres	MGMT

In this case student Lopez has not chosen a major. Consider the question; *Find all students who are not MIS majors.* The following query is the natural response:

> SELECT same
> FROM Students
> WHERE major != 'MIS';

The results are:

Notice that *Lopez* is not in the result set. It is clear that *Lopez* does not have *MIS* for a *major*. Why then does *Lopez* not appear in the results? Remember that *SQL* will return the *sname* from all rows for which *major != 'MIS'* is *True*. For the *Lopez* row, the expression *major != 'MIS'* has the value *Null*! The row is skipped. This query found those *students* whose *major* is known to not be *MIS*. To find those *students* whose *major* is not known to be *MIS* the following query is needed:

> SELECT same
> FROM Students
> WHERE major != 'MIS'
>   OR major is Null ;

The results are:

It is not likely that the average user will be sufficiently aware of this issue. In fact, it will take most users some time to grasp the difference between finding those *students* whose *major* is known to not be *MIS*, and finding those *students* whose *major* is not known to be *MIS*. Further, it is often not clear which of these two questions will satisfy the actual requirement. For this reason it is recommended that *Nulls* not be allowed in columns that may be involved in queries that involve "NOT".

Nulls in Summaries

When a column that accepts Null appears in a summary function, (SUM, AVG, MIN, MAX) all null values in the column are ignored in the computation of the summary. This is what the user might expect. The COUNT summary function behaves differently with Nulls. Consider again the table:

Students

sn	sname	major
S1	Smith	MIS
S2	Doe	MGMT
S3	Lopez	Null
S4	Chen	ECON
S5	Dupres	MGMT

To find the number of students the following query works well:

SELECY COUNT(*) AS TOTAL
FROM Students;

The results are:

TOTAL
5

To find the number of students who have selected a major one would replace the asterisk with *major*. In this case the number of rows where *major* has a value is counted. The query is:

SELECY COUNT(major) AS TOTAL
FROM Students;

The results are:

In summary, *Null* is a useful value in situations where a value may be unknown, may not exist, or may be inappropriate. *Nulls* are dangerous in columns that are involved in expressions in *WHERE* clauses that involve *NOT*. Further, the use of *Nulls* in numeric columns may make the use of summaries unpredictable. Finally the *Count* summary ignores *Null* values when a specific column is supplied, however when '*' is used as the argument, the total number of rows is determined regardless of their contents.

Default Values

Since the concept of *Null* can have some unexpected results, yet missing data values can be reasonably expected, there is another feature implemented in many relational database management systems. This is the *default value*. This is a specific entry that has a value and data type that the DBA would specify to be used for a column when a row is created and no value is specified for the column. Since the default value has a data type and a value all of the issues that led to three valued logic disappear. However, since the entry will have a value, it is included in summaries. Therefore, if, for example zero is used for missing values of the attribute *age*, then the summary *AVERAGE(age)* will produce a smaller value than is expected if there are any missing values. Once again, the DBA must make these decisions carefully, and communicate carefully with the users about how these decisions might affect the queries users might write.

5 TRANSACTIONS

The Transaction

Up to this point all of the *SQL* statements written have been
considered to be independent and singular. That is, they perform a
simple single task. It is possible to define a task that requires more
than one *SQL* statement. If the task is to be performed successfully
all of the statements must be performed successfully. If not, then
none of the statements may be performed. For example, to transfer
$10.00 from account A to account B requires two *UPDATE*
statements:

> UPDATE Accounts
> SET Balance = Balance – 10
> WHERE Account = 'A';

and

> UPDATE Accounts
> SET Balance = Balance + 10
> WHERE Account = 'B';

It is clear that if it is possible for only one of these statements to
succeed for any reason then funds may either be lost or gained

inappropriately. Therefore it is imperative that a mechanism to ensure that either both succeed or neither succeed. This is the purpose of the transaction. A transaction is defined as a logical unit of work that must succeed completely or be entirely undone. To implement transactions in *SQL*, two *SQL* commands are used, *COMMIT* and *ROLLBACK*. There is actually a third command, *BEGIN TRANSACTION* that is implicit in all *DDL* and *DML* commands, so its use is redundant. The *BEGIN TRANSACTION* command causes a transaction to begin. If no transaction is in progress for the current session, then any *DDL* or *DML* statement will generate a *BEGIN TRANSACTION*. If a transaction is in progress, then no new *BEGIN TRANSACTION* is entered. The commands *COMMIT* and *ROLLBACK* each signal the end of a transaction. The *COMMIT* command ends a transaction and makes permanent all of the database changes contained in the transaction. The *ROLLBACK* command will undo all changes to the database made in this transaction. This is possible because all changes to the database are recorded in a rollback file or space. The transaction ID and all pre-images of the updated records are stored in the order they are recorded. The *ROLLBACK* merely applies the pre-images to the database in the reverse order they were executed in the transaction, thereby leaving the database in the same condition after the transaction as it was at the start of the transaction.

Using the conventional *GO TO* style coding for error handlers, the above *UPDATE* statements can be incorporated into a transaction. Pseudocode for the transaction is:

```
UPDATE Accounts

SET Balance = Balance – 10

WHERE Account = 'A';


IF errors THEN GOTO UNDO


UPDATE Accounts

SET Balance = Balance + 10

WHERE Account = 'B';


IF errors THEN GOTO UNDO
```

In this example the transaction begins with the *BEGIN TRANSACTION* and finishes with either the *COMMIT* or the *ROLLBACK* command.

There are cases where a single *SQL* statement will behave like a transaction in that the statement causes the update of many records. It is not acceptable that only some of the records get updated. All chosen records must be updated or none may be updated. Consider the example where the *balance* is to be reduced by 1.00 for every account where the *fee* field is 'Y'. The following *SQL* will accomplish this.

```
UPDATE Accounts
SET Balance = Balance – 1
WHERE Fee = 'Y';
```

If there is a constraint on *Balance* so that it may not be less than zero for any *Account*, then if during the update of the *Accounts* an *Account* has a beginning balance of zero this *UPDATE* will cause an error. That *Balance* will not be updated. Therefore all of the other *Balance* values that have already been changed by this statement must be rolled back.

Another interesting case where a single *UPDATE* may cause a *ROLLBACK* is the case where a foreign key value is updated or deleted, and referential integrity is maintained through *CASCADE*. In this case the initial update/delete will cause changes in other records. If an error occurs in one of these consequential updates/deletes, all of the updates/deletes must be rolled back.

Recovery From System Failure

The previous section demonstrated methods to manage maintaining consistency of the DBMS when errors were trapped or detected by the application. In this case the application is still in control, and can issue a *COMMIT* or a *ROLLBACK*. Consider the case that some part of the environment fails, that is, the DBMS, the application hardware or software, the operating system or the network fails. In this case any transaction that is still in progress must be considered to have failed since it is not known what further work would have been done. Any work done by that transaction will need to be removed from the database. This is complicated further by the fact that in order to gain acceptable levels of performance, Input/Output buffering is employed by the DBMS. Therefore, even though a transaction may have successfully written data, the data may still be resident in an output buffer awaiting the actual hardware I/O operation. In this case since data in buffers will be lost, the database will not see this change, and the database will not be consistent after the failure. There is a clever process used universally by DBMS developers in some form or other that will allow for recovery of the database to a consistent state after a failure.

While a discussion about the recovery mechanism of a DBMS has no immediate relevance to the *SQL* user or application developer, it will provide some insight into the ways that a DBMS provides protection for data. This discussion will provide some insight to the DBA in the setup of the DBMS environment including things like the location and size of the log file.

The recovery process is centered on the log file (sometimes called a journal). This is a file usually kept on a separate medium from the database, and often mirrored on a second location. The important issue is that if the database itself is physically harmed, at least one copy of the log file will not be harmed. The log file is a sequential record of all activity on the database. For performance sake, the log file often only records database writes and updates to the database since these are all that is needed for recovery. When security and auditing of database access is important, the log can also record all database reads. This decision is made by the DBA and set as an operational parameter of the DBMS. Each entry in the log will contain a transaction ID, the pre-image of the update and a post-image of the update. Since the log file is likely to be active, good performance will necessitate buffering the log file writes. In order for the log file to be useful in the recovery process it is essential that the *write-ahead log rule* be enforced. This rule states that before a transaction completes all buffered log entries for the transaction must be physically written to the log. Note that the database data may still be in database buffers or may have been physically written to the database. In either case, the log contains a complete record of the work done for any completed transaction. For transactions that are in progress there may be database data and log entries that are buffered. In order for the recovery process to work it will be essential for there to be points in time when the physical database and the log file are completely consistent, that there is nothing in either the database buffers or the log buffer. This is called a log checkpoint. At a specified interval, all database processing is frozen so that no new data is placed in buffers, then all buffers are physically written, then a checkpoint record including the IDs of all currently executing transactions is written, then the DBMS is allowed to resume processing. The frequency of checkpoint writing can be determined by the DBA. There is a trade-off between the performance loss in performing checkpoints, and the amount of effort requires accomplishing a recovery. This trade-off governs decisions by the DBA in setting this interval. A longer interval improves performance, but lengthens the recovery process. A shorter interval requires more checkpoints thereby impacting performance, but recovery is quicker.

There are five different possible conditions that a transaction can be in at the time of a system failure. They are:

1. The transaction completed prior to the last checkpoint.
   In this case the execution of the checkpoint would have ensured that all of the work of the transaction was physically written to the database. In this case there is nothing to recover. This transaction can be ignored.

2. The transaction started prior to the last checkpoint and completed prior to the system failure.
   In this case the transaction completed correctly, however some of the data may not have been moved from buffers to the database. All of the data exists on the log, so this transaction can be *re-done*.

3. The transaction started prior to the last checkpoint and never finished.
   In this case the transaction never completed, so it is not known how it would complete. Therefore the transaction must be *un-done*. This will entail restoring some data on the database to original values.

4. The transaction started after the last checkpoint and finished before the failure.
   This case is similar to case 2. Since the transaction completed, all of the work of the transaction exists on the log. Even though some (maybe all) of the work was not written to the database, this transaction is recoverable. It must be *re-done*.

5. The transaction started after the last checkpoint and never finished.
   Since this transaction never finished it must be *un-done*. This may be moot since it is possible that none of the work was ever written to the database.

There is a simple algorithm used to process the log file after a failure to determine which transactions must be *re-done* and which must be *un-done*, and in fact accomplish the re-do and un-do processes. The first step is to determine which transactions are to be re-done and which are to be undone. The all transactions are undone by writing the pre-images from the log for all database writes, then the transactions to be re-done are re-done by writing all of the post-images from the log for those transactions to be re-done. The pseudocode for this algorithm is:

```
BEGIN RECOVERY
Declare Un-do and Re-do lists;
READING BACKWARD ON LOG

REPEAT UNTIL log-entry is checkpoint;

Place all active transactions at checkpoint
on Un-do list;

READING FORWARD ON LOG

REPEAT UNTIL end-of-log

        IF log entry is end-of transaction THEN
                Move transaction from un-do list to re-do
                list;

        IF log entry is start-of-transaction THEN
                Add transaction to un-do list;
END REPEAT;
READING BACKWARD ON LOG

REPEAT UNTIL event is start of earliest transaction on un-do
list

        IF event is a database write THEN
                WRITE the pre-image;

END REPEAT;

READING FORWARD ON LOG
REPEAT UNTIL end-of-log

        IF event is a database write
            AND
            transaction on re-do list THEN
                WRITE post images;

END REPEAT
END RECOVERY
```

In older implementations of databases where the log file was kept on a magnetic tape, the progress of this algorithm could be observed as the tape slowly wound backward then forward, then backward again and finally forward.

6 SQL IN APPLICATIONS

Embedded SQL

It is often important for an application written in a traditional sequential programming language like COBOL, C++, MS Visual Basic, or JAVA to need to process information in a database. Further it will be important for the application to be allowed to construct the query to be used at application run time. The basic difference between these sequential prescriptive languages and the descriptive language *SQL* complicates this process a bit. An *SQL* query will produce an entire table of results, whereas a sequential language will be able to handle only simple values. The sequential language will want to process the table one row at a time. A further complication comes from the fact that the internal data storage data types and formats are not necessarily the same as the internal data format of the DBMS. In order to accommodate these needs the producers of DBMS software have developed language specific compiler extensions called embedded SQL. These extensions allow for definition of application variables that can hold and communicate data from fields in the DBMS. The extensions also define cursors that facilitate the processing of a table in an application. There is also error and state information that is exchanged so that an application can detect when a query generates an error and react responsively.

The principal difficulty with embedded *SQL* is that it is developed as compiler extensions. Therefore an implementation of embedded *SQL* must be developed for each compiler. In addition, the application code is linked at compile time to a specific DBMS. This does not allow for an acceptable level of flexibility. While embedded *SQL* is a part of the *SQL* standard, and most DBMS developers have implemented the extensions for the popular programming languages, it is clear that a more flexible solution such as a call level interface is needed. The Microsoft Open Database Connectivity Application Programming Interface, ODBC API provides this flexibility. The reader who is interested in further information on Embedded or Dynamic SQL is encouraged to consult the fine reference on the *SQL* standard by Date and Darwen[5].

The ODBC API and JDBC API

The ODBC API is a library of functions that allows an application to access a DBMS using *SQL*. The JDBC API is a library with similar functionality developed specifically for the Java development environment. The interface is designed to appear implementation neutral so applications can be developed without specific concern about the implementation details of the DBMS to be accessed. This is made possible by placing the implementation specific characteristics in interfaces called ODBC drivers. Each DBMS implementation has its own ODBC driver. The task of choosing and loading the particular driver needed by an application is that of the Driver Manager. The interface is also designed so that it is productive in a wide variety of application development environments. The ODBC API has four essential functional parts, the application, the driver manager, the driver and the DBMS.

The functions to be performed by the drivers can be grouped into the following groupings:

---

[5] A Guide to the SQL Standard 4th ed., C. J. Date and H. Darwen, Addison Wesley, 1997.

- **Managing connections.** All of the necessary allocations and deallocations of memory and storage are made. This includes environment or global information and connection specific information such as login ID and password. The drivers establish connections, validate security information, and provide for different types of access such as read-only, read-write, etc.

- **Performing Queries and Retrieving Results.** The drivers must provide a mechanism for sending a query to the DBMS and receiving the results of the query. This also includes providing tools for the application to use to view the results in a productive way.

- **Transaction Control.** The value of transactions in a shared environment has been demonstrated. It is essential that tools for establishing and controlling transactions be available through the ODBC drivers.

- **Error Management.** The fact that the ODBC drivers allow application developers to write programs that control actions taken in a remote DBMS forces the application developer to take control of the myriad of conditions that can arise. Therefore a major role of the driver is to pass error and control information from the DBMS to the application.

In its simplest form, an application using ODBC to obtain information from a database will: open a connection to the database, form a statement that describes the SQL to be executed, retrieve and process the desired results and handle any errors that may result. The example below is code from a simple MS Visual Basic program. This is the code that when executed will retrieve all of the values from the *Parts* table from the *PartsDB.mdb* database, and display the contents of the second column of the table in a ListBox named list1.

```
Private Sub Command1_Click()
Dim myConnection As New ADODB.Connection
Dim myRecordset As ADODB.Recordset
'
'Establish the Connection String
'
myConnection.ConnectionString =_
    Provider=Microsoft.Jet.OLEDB.4.0;" _
 & "Data Source=pathtodatabase\PartsDB.mdb;" _
 & "Persist Security Info=False"
'
' Open the Connection
'
myConnection.Open
'
' Trap and Handle SQL errors
'
On Error GoTo ErrHandler
'
' Send the SQL and retrieve the records
'
Set myRecordset =_
    myConnection.Execute("select * from parts")

'
' Process the records
'
myRecordset.MoveFirst
Do While Not myRecordset.EOF
    List1.AddItem myRecordset(1)
    myRecordset.MoveNext
Loop
On Error GoTo 0
'
' Close the connection
'
myConnection.Close
Exit Sub
ErrHandler:
'
' Show the description of the error in a Message Box
'
ret1 = MsgBox(myConnection.Errors(0).Description)
End Sub
```

The following segment of a JAVA Applet using JDBC shows the *sname* data from the *Students* table would be extracted from a database and placed in a list named *ll* using a resultset *rs1* and the implicitly defined cursor and the *next* method of the resultset. The database is an ORACLE® database on an Internet server. This Applet segment is included as a demonstration of the cursor concept, and not as a learning exercise. The JAVA language concepts and subtleties are beyond the scope of this work.

```
import java.awt.*;
import java.awt.event.*;
import java.applet.*;
import java.sql.*;
import oracle.jdbc.driver.*;
public class MyOracle extends Applet implements
        ActionListener
{
     private Button b1;
     private List l1;
     private Connection c1;
     private Statement s1;
     private ResultSet rs1;
     public void init()
     {
         this.setLayout( new FlowLayout());
         b1=new Button("Read");
         b1.addActionListener(this);
         this.add(b1);
         l1=new List(5);
         this.add(l1);
     }

     public void actionPerformed(ActionEvent e1)
     {
         if(e1.getSource() == b1)
         {
             this.showStatus("Connecting....");
             try
             {
               DriverManager.registerDriver(
               new oracle.jdbc.driver.OracleDriver());
                 String dbconn=
    "(DESCRIPTION=(ADDRESS=(HOST=Internet address)"
                 + "(PROTOCOL=TCP) (PORT=nnnn))"
               + "(CONNECT_DATA=(SID=XXXX)))";
               c1=DriverManager.getConnection(
               "jdbc:oracle:thin:@"

                                  + dbconn ,"UID","PWD");

                 c1.setAutoCommit(true);
                 this.showStatus("Connected");
             }
             catch(Throwable e2)
             {
                 this.showStatus(e2.toString());
             }


                     .
                     .
                     .
```

```
try
{
        s1=c1.createStatement();

        rs1=s1.executeQuery("select * from students");
        ll.clear();
        while( rs1.next())
        {
            ll.addItem(rs1.getString(1));
        }
        c1.close();
        this.showStatus("Connection Closed");
```

Note in this example the line of code:
c1.setAutoCommit(true); This code tells the ORACLE®
DBMS that the program does not wish to have explicit transaction
control. Therefore the DBMS will issue a *COMMIT* implicitly
after each *SQL* command. In this case since the *SQL* only reads
the database there is no impact.

7 THE RELATIONAL DATABASE

Introduction

The SQL exercises have shown that a relational database looks like a collection of tables of data. This is an excellent first image of a database. This image or picture of a database falls quite short of explaining some of the important features of a database. In particular, how is it possible for a relational database to model business rules for an application system? The answer is that there are some important structural rules that must be followed in the construction and maintenance of tables. This chapter will develop the relational database framework. There will be many important terms and concepts defined. A good understanding of these terms is essential to the ability to design and maintain a functional database.

The Relational Table

A relational table is a set of column definitions or attributes together with a time-varying collection of zero or more rows. A column definition is, at least, a column name, a data type and a statement as to whether the column may accept *Nulls*. In many implementations of SQL column definitions have further properties such as value constraints, display formats, size constraints, etc. This set of column definitions are established when a table is created using a *CREATE* statement. The set may be modified using the *ALTER TABLE* statement. Note that it is only possible to add new columns and delete columns. One cannot reasonably expect to change the type of a column. The time varying set of rows of a table are added to using the *INSERT* statement, removed from using the *DELETE* statement, and changed using the *UPDATE* statement.

There are five essential properties of a table. These properties guide the way in which a user might use a table. They are:

1. *All values in a table are explicit.* No value is represented as a formula or a reference to some other object or set of objects. The values in a row of a table do not depend on any other row in the table, nor do they depend on values in any other table.
2. *All values are atomic.* No value can be further sub-divided. Care must be taken here to understand the principle here. While there are functions that may extract or reference a part of a value, e.g. the *substring* function, the value is inserted and updated as a whole.
3. *No duplicate rows.* It is not possible to have two rows that are exactly the same. If there were tow rows that were the same, then it would be impossible to decide which one to ally a change to, or to delete. Further, since the rows represent instances of the entity that the table represents, two different rows represent two different instances of the entity. If all the attributes in the table for these two rows are the same, then there is some other distinguishing attribute for these rows that should also be included in the table.
4. *The rows are stored inherently unordered.* Often the rows will be displayed when a *SELECT* statement is used in either the order they are entered, or in order by the primary key. (This term will be defined carefully below.) This is because the SQL engine finds it most convenient to do so. A table must be considered as a *set* of rows. Therefore there is no concept of first row, last row, n^{th} row, next row

or previous row. Since it is often necessary to view the rows in a given order, or to process the rows in embedded SQL in a given order, the *SELECT* statement has an *ORDER BY* clause to present the rows in a given order. The rows are, however stored in no specific order.

5. *The columns are referenced by name.* It is not possible in *SQL* to *SELECT* the first three columns, or to *UPATE* every other column or perform other such operations on indefinite sets of columns. This is relaxed a bit for the embedded *SQL* implementations. Most implementations allow the columns to be referenced by a column index that is established by the order in which the columns were defined.

Keys and Integrity Rules

The concept of key is central to making a set of tables conform to the business rules of the application system.

Candidate Key

A candidate key is an attribute or set of attributes that can act as a unique identifier of rows in a table. Specifically, a candidate key must have:

- *Uniqueness.* All rows in the table are unique in the(se) attribute(s) according to some business rule.
- *Minimality.* If the key consists of more than one attribute, then no attribute can be removed and have uniqueness exist.

Consider the *Students* table. It has the attributes *sn, sname,* and *major*. At first glance, both *sn* and *sname* appear to be unique. This is a consequence of the data values, and not a business rule. A business rule would be that the student numbers are unique, however there could be no business rule to indicate that the students name is unique. It would be very reasonable to have two students named *Smith*. Therefore *sn* is the only reasonable candidate key. Since *sn* is a unique identifier, it is clear that any set of attributes that contains *sn* will also be a unique identifier. This is where minimality is important. Minimality would not allow any of these combinations to be a candidate key.

Because one of the properties of a table is that there are no duplicate rows, a little thought will lead to the fact that every table has a candidate key. In some tables such as *Students* the candidate key is a single attribute. In other tables like *Registrations* the candidate key is formed using all of the attributes.

Consider now the following modification to the *Students* table. Add the attribute *ssn*, which stands for social security number. There is a business rule indicating that *sn* be unique. There is another business rule that indicates that *ssn* be unique. There are two different minimal unique identifiers for this modified *Students* table. This *Students* table has two different candidate keys. This is completely reasonable. For this reason it is necessary to define the primary key.

Primary Key
The primary key of a table is the candidate key chosen by the DBA. This will be the candidate key that is used to reference other tables. In the case of the *Students* table, the logical choice for primary key is *sn*.

Alternate Key
This is a term used to reference any candidate key that is not a primary key. There is no role for alternate keys in the design of databases. The term is included here for the sake of completeness.

The most important task of a primary key is to be a unique identifier for a table. That is, it should be possible to reference any single specific row in a table using the primary key. Consider what happens when the primary key is allowed to contain *Nulls*. Remember from the discussion of *Null* that *Null* = *Null* is not true. Therefore two different rows of a table could have *Null* in the primary key and uniqueness would still be satisfied. The primary key would become useless as a unique identifier. It is for this reason that entity integrity is defined.

Look now at the tables in the Students database. Again, it is clear that the only candidate key in *Students* is *sn*. Therefore sn is the primary key of *Students*. In a similar way, the only candidate keys for *Courses* and *Teachers* are *cn* and *tn* respectively. Therefore the primary key of *Courses* is *cn*, and the primary key of *Teachers* is *tn*. The *Registrations* table is a bit trickier. Clearly neither *sn* nor *cn* have uniqueness. However, together the pair (*sn, cn*) is unique. Each row in *Registrations* represents the registration of a student in a course. The primary key of *Registrations* is the combined attribute (*sn, cn*).

Entity Integrity
The primary key of a table may not be *Null*.

This is so important in making a primary key useful that many implementations of SQL will automatically ensure that the attribute(s) chosen for a candidate key is(are) not allowed to be *Null*. This however, should not be assumed. The clause *NOT NULL* should be placed in the attribute definition for all attributes participating in the primary key. Following is the SQL to appropriately create the *Students* table, and the primary key constraint.

```
CREATE TABLE Students(
    sn   VARCHAR(5)   NOT NULL,
    sname   VARCHAR(15),
    major   VARCHAR(4),
        PRIMARY KEY sn);
```

The concept of *foreign key* is central to the database design process. The *primary key* and *entity integrity* form rules about the nature of a single table. The *foreign key* and *referential integrity* form rules about how tables in a database relate to each other.

Foreign Key
An attribute or set of attributes in one table that obtains its values from the primary key of another table is a *foreign key*.

Not all tables will contain a foreign key, and some tables may have more than one foreign keyIn the *Students* database it is clear that the *Students* table and the *Teachers* table do not have foreign keys. None of the columns in these tables derive their values from the primary keys of other tables. In courses, however, the column *tn* derives its values from the primary key of *Teachers*. The column *tn* in *Courses* is a foreign key on *Teachers*. In the *Registrations* table each of the columns *sn* and *cn* derive their values from the primary keys of other tables. Therefore, *sn* is a foreign key on *Students* and *cn* is a foreign key on *Courses*. The table *Registrations* has two foreign keys.

There is one other special case of the use of a foreign key. It is possible for a one column or set of columns in a table to be foreign key on the same table. For example, consider this extension to *Students*. Add the column *Roommate*. The values in this column are chosen from the *Students*. The *Roomate* column draws its values from the primary key of *Students*, so it is a foreign key on *Sn* in *Students*. This table holds information about companies. The primary key is *cid* or company id. A student that has no roomate would have *Null* in the *Roomate* field.

Referential Integrity
All of the values in a foreign key column(s) must be represented in the corresponding primary key column(s), or be entirely *Null*.

In simple terms this says that there cannot be a *Registration* for a *Student* that does not exist, or for a *Course* that does not exist. Also, a *Course* may not be taught by a *Teacher* that does not exist. In the *Courses* table there could exist a row for a course with no *Teacher* assigned. The value in the *tn* column for that row would be *Null*. This is permissible within referential integrity. Since *sn* and *cn* are both part of the primary key for *Registrations*, neither can be *Null*. Therefore, if a *Registration* row exists it must be for an existing *Student* and an existing *Course*.

As a foreign key is established referential integrity is automatically enforced by the DBMS. There are different ways in which this enforcement can be handled, and these will be presented below. The following syntax is the *SQL* to establish the foreign keys in the *Registrations* table:

```
CREATE TABLE Registrations(
    sn  VARCHAR(5)   NOT NULL,
    cn  VARCHAR(5)   NOT NULL,
        PRIMARY KEY sn,cn,
        FOREIGN KEY sn REFERENCES
Students (sn),
        FOREIGN KEY cn REFERENCES Courses
(cn));
```

An alternate syntax is available to make a column a primary key or a foreign key if the table already exists. With this new syntax the developer creates the constraint explicitly the the primary key and the foreign key. This makes use of the ALTER TABLE syntax.

```
ALTER TABLE Registrations
    ADD CONSTRAINT STUD_PK
PRIMARY KEY(sn);

ALTER TABLE REGISTRATIONS
    ADD CONSTRAINT
```

REG_STUD_FK FOREIGN KEY (sn)
REFERENCES STUDENTS(sn);

There are four different ways to maintain referential integrity between the foreign key and the primary key values as the rows in the database are changed and deleted. These are *restricting, cascading setting to default, and nullifying.* Further different methods can be specified for deletes and for updates. While these will all be discussed here, not all implementations of *SQL* implement all four.

Restricting
This is the simplest method. It merely says that if a change to the database that will break referential integrity is requested, it is blocked. A message to the user or application program is provided. For example, if a row with a non-existent *Student* is inserted into *Registrations* the INSERT will be halted and a message will be returned. If the *sn* for a *student* is changed, and the *student* has *Registration* rows, then the change will be blocked and a message will be returned. If an attempt to delete a *Student* row that has corresponding *Registration* rows, the delete will be blocked and a message will be returned.

Cascading
In this method changes in primary key values that would cause problems with referential integrity are propagated to the foreign key. If a *Students sn* is changed, then that same change is made in every *Registration* that referenced the *Student*. If a *Student* row is deleted, then every *Registration* that references the *Student* is deleted. Further, the delete is cascaded to any other table that might have (*sn, cn*) as a foreign key.

Setting to Default and Nullifying
In this method, when a change is made in a primary key value, any resulting entries in the corresponding foreign keys are replaced

with either the default value or *Nulls*. If replacing a foreign key value with a default value or *Null* would cause an entity integrity problem, then the change is blocked and a message is returned to the user or application program.

The syntax to set up the foreign keys *sn* and *cn* in *Registrations* so that updates are cascaded, and deletes are restricted follows. In this case, changes to student numbers or course numbers in *Students* and *Courses* would be propagated to *Registrations*, however no *Student* and no *Course* can be deleted as long as there are corresponding *Registrations*.

```
CREATE TABLE Registrations(
    sn   VARCHAR(5)   NOT NULL,
    cn   VARCHAR(5)   NOT NULL,
    PRIMARY KEY sn,cn,
    FOREIGN KEY sn REFERENCES
Students (sn)
        ON DELETE NO ACTION
        ON UPDATE CASCADE,
    FOREIGN KEY cn REFERENCES Courses
(cn)
        ON DELETE NO ACTION
        ON UPDATE CASCADE);
```

8 NORMALIZATION

Introduction

In a database a relational table will represent a business entity of some type. The attributes of the entity will serve to describe the entity, and the rows of the table will represent instances of the entity. The operations available in the relational model allow rows to be added, removed, changed and selected from the table as needed. It is important that the rows be structured so that none of these operations are context sensitive or value sensitive. That is, one should not have to look at the content of a row to decide how to insert, delete, update, select or perform any other operation with it. This is the basic purpose of normalization.

There are several normal forms, 1NF, 2NF, 3NF, BCNF, 4NF and 5NF. Each successive NF resolves a design issue with data tables that was left with the previous normal form. Further each normal form includes the previous form. That is to say, if a table is 2NF, then it is 1NF; if it is 3NF then it is 2NF, etc. The normal forms were developed by researchers sequentially. They will be presented in the order they were developed. In this way, the reader will gain more insight into the entire process of normalization.

As each normal form is presented, some sample problems with tables that are not in this normal form will be discussed. These will be presented as update anomalies. It is through these update anomalies that the nature of the design issues resolved by normalization will be seen.

The normal forms describe restrictions on the way in which the attributes in a table relate to each other. These relationships will be defined in terms of functional dependencies. The discussion of normalization will begin with an understanding of functional dependencies.

Functional Dependency

The relationships between the attributes of a table are defined by functional dependencies.

Functional Dependency
The attribute *b* is functionally dependant on the set of attributes *a* if for each value of *a* there is exactly one value of *b* by some business rule. Alternatively, it can be said that the set of attributes *a* functionally determines the attribute *b*. This is often denoted by the diagram:

$$a \longrightarrow b$$

To provide an example of this concept, consider the table *Students*. It is clear that for each value of the attribute *sn* there is only one value of *sname* and one value of *major*. On the other hand, for each value of *sname* there may be more than one *sn*. After all there is no business rule stating that there cannot be students with the same name. Further, it is likely that there will be more than one *sn* for each *major*. Therefore for the attributes in *Students* the following functional dependencies hold:

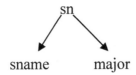

It is not always necessary for there to be any functional dependencies among the attributes of a table. Consider the table *Registrations*. In this table neither of the attributes *sn* nor *cn* determine the other. This table has no functional dependencies among the attributes.

First Normal Form, 1NF

A table is in 1NF if and only if all of the functional dependencies determine atomic attributes. That is, if *a* determines *b*, then *b* is a simple attribute with no internal structure. The determinant *b* cannot be a repeating group of attributes or a table or any other type of structure of attributes. Consider the following example:

ZeroA

Sn	Cna	Cnb	Cnc	Cnd	Cne	Cnf
S1	C1	C2	C3	C4	C5	*null*
S2	C2	C4	*null*	*null*	*null*	*null*
S3	C3	*null*	*null*	*null*	*null*	*null*

Each value of *sn* determines a collection of *cn* values. In this case *can*, *cnb*, *cnc*, *cnd*, *cne*, and *cnf* form a repeating group. The table *ZeroA* is not 1NF. Consider this alternate form of the table:

ZeroB

Sn	Cn
	C1
	C2
S1	C3
	C4
	C5
S2	C2
	C4
S3	C3

In this table *sn* actually determines a table. That is, the values of
the attribute *cn* are tables themselves. The table *ZeroB* is also not
1NF.

Adding a registration to *ZeroA* or *ZeroB* for the pair (*S2, C4*) will
require that the row for *S2* be updated. On the other hand, adding a
registration for the pair (*S4, C1*) will require that a new row be
inserted. Similarly, deleting the registration (*S1,C4*) will require
an update to the *S1* row, while deleting the registration for (*S3,C3*)
will require that a row be deleted. It is easy to see in this case that
the processes for inserting and deleting data for the tables *ZeroA*
and *ZeroB* are dependant on the values of the data that is in the
table. This is an unacceptable update anomaly.

The same information that is contained in either *ZeroA* or *ZeroB*
can be represented in a 1NF table by distributing the value of *Sn* to
each of the *Cn* values. The table becomes the familiar
Registrations table. This table is 1NF.

Registrations

sn	cn
S1	C1
S1	C2
S1	C3
S1	C4
S1	C5
S2	C2
S2	C4
S3	C3

Second Normal Form, 2NF

A table is 2NF if and only if it is 1NF, and every non-key attribute
is FD on a candidate key.
Consider now the following table:

One

sn	cn	sname	major
S1	C1	Smith	MIS
S1	C2	Smith	MIS
S1	C3	Smith	MIS
S1	C4	Smith	MIS
S1	C5	Smith	MIS
S2	C2	Doe	MGMT
S2	C4	Doe	MGMT
S3	C3	Lopez	MIS

In this table, the attribute pair *(sn, cn)* is the primary key. The functional dependencies among the attributes of this table can be represented as:

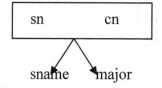

In this table, the non-key attributes *sname* and *major* are FD on only the attribute *sn*. They are not FD on the candidate key. This table is not 2NF.

There are a number of update anomalies with this table. If one were to update the *major* value for the row with key value *(S1, C1)* to *ECON*, there would be an inconsistency in major values for *S1*. In four of the rows the value is *MIS*, and in one row it is *ECON*. This is unacceptable. If one were to attempt to insert information for Student *S4*, *(S4, Chen, ECON)* the attempt would be blocked. Since there is no value for *Cn*, *Null* would be used, and the key cannot contain a *Null* value. It is not possible to add a *Student* until the *Student* actually registers for a class. Finally, if one were to delete the row for *(S3, C3)* one would lose all *sname* and *major* information. This also is unacceptable. The underlying reason for these anomalies is that the table *One* is actually representing two different business entities, *Students* and *Registrations*. This table must be split into two tables. One table (*Students*) with key *sn* and attributes *sname* and *major*, and another table (*Registrations*) with key (*sn, cn*). This table is all key. These tables will be 2NF. The following SQL accomplishes this.

CREATE TABLE Students AS SELECT DISTINCT sn, sname, major FROM One;

CREATE TABLE Registrations AS SELECT DISTINCT sn, cn FROM One;

Students

sn	sname	major
S1	Smith	MIS
S2	Doe	MGMT
S3	Lopez	MIS

Registrations

sn	cn
S1	C1
S1	C2
S1	C3
S1	C4
S1	C5
S2	C2
S2	C4
S3	C3

If necessary, to retain data independence, the original table *One* can be recovered as a view which is the *INNER JOIN* of the *Students* and *Registrations* tables on the *sn* column in each. Every 1NF table that is not 2NF can be divided into as many tables as there are groupings of FDs, and recombined with a corresponding set of *INNER JOIN*s on the new key attributes.

Third Normal Form, 3NF

A table is 3NF if and only if it is 2NF and all non-key attributes are non-transitively FD on a candidate key.

Consider now the following table:

Two						
sn	*sname*	*major*	*street*	*city*	*state*	*zip*
S1	Smith	MIS	123 Main	Houston	TX	77002
S2	Doe	MGMT	234 Elm	Austin	TX	75123
S3	Lopez	MIS	543 Pine	Spring	TX	77059
S4	Chen	ECON	456 Oak	Dallas	TX	72012
S5	Dupres	MGMT	765 Fir	Houston	TX	77002

The primary key for this table is *sn*, and the FDs for the attributes are as follows:

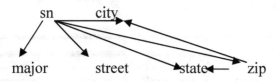

It is clear that *sn* determines all of the attributes. However, the postal system has defined business rules where *zip* determines both *city* and *state*. Actually, the 9-digit *zip* also determines *street*. For simplicity assume *Zip* is a 5-digit zip. The attribute *city* does not determine *state*. There is a *Santa Fe* in CA, NM and TX, among numerous other examples. All attributes except *sn* are non-key, and all are FD on the candidate key. Therefore *Two* is 2NF. The FDs *sn* → *city* and *sn* → *state* are actually derived FDs. Because *sn* → *zip* and *zip* → *city*, then *sn* → *city* transitively. The same is true for *sn* → *state*. Therefore the attributes *city* and *state* are transitively FD on the candidate key. This table is not 3NF.

The update anomalies arise in this case because this table contains two different business rules. The table contains demographic information about students, and the table contains the postal system routing information. These can change independently. Consider the case that *S3* must change city to *Houston* because the city of *Houston* annexed the village of *Spring*. In this case the change would need to be made in all rows that have *zip* equal to *79959*. However in the case that *S3* must change *major*, only the *S3* row will be affected. The method of performing updates for this table will depend on the nature of the update. This is unacceptable. Inserting a new row in this table will require validation of the *zip*, *city*, and *state* values with the postal routing system in order to avoid inconsistent data in the table. This is also unacceptable. The table *Two* must be split into two tables, one representing student information, *sn, sname, major, street, zip*, and one containing the postal routing information, *zip, city,* and *state*.

```
CREATE TABLE Students AS
SELECT DISTINCT sn, sname, major, street, zip
FROM Two;
```
Students

sn	sname	major	street	zip
S1	Smith	MIS	123 Main	77002
S2	Doe	MGMT	234 Elm	75123
S3	Lopez	MIS	543 Pine	77059
S4	Chen	ECON	456 Oak	72012
S5	Dupres	MGMT	765 Fir	77002

```
CREATE TABLE Postal AS
SELECT DISTINCT zip, city, state
FROM One;
```
Postal

zip	city	state
77002	Houston	TX
75123	Austin	TX
77059	Spring	TX
72012	Dallas	TX

As before, if it is necessary to retain data independence, the original table *Two* can be recovered as a view that is the INNER

JOIN of the Students and *Postal* tables on the *zip* column in each. Every 2NF table that is not 3NF can be divided into as many tables as there are groupings of transitive FDs, and recombined with a corresponding set of *INNER JOINs* on the new key attributes.

It is important to be careful deciding how to split the attributes. The split must be done so that every FD in the original table can be deduced from the FDs in the split tables, and so that all attributes that are common to the split tables form a candidate key of one of the split tables. In the above case it is clear that all of the FDs in the original table can be derived from the FDs of the split tables, and the only common attribute is *Zip*, which forms the candidate key of *Postal*.

It is clear that the process of normalizing is the process of reducing all tables to simple entities that embody only one simple business rule. For most entities one can imagine, 3NF is sufficient. Third Normal Form does not, however, address some special cases. The first case is where there are intra key FDs, or where there are FDs that determine a key attribute. These are admittedly rare, but not impossible. The Boyce-Codd Normal Form was developed to deal with this case.

Boyce-Codd Normal Form, BCNF

A table is BCNF if and only if <u>all</u> FDs are generated by a candidate key.

Consider this table:

Three

sn	ssn	cn	date
S1	123-45-6789	C1	7/21/03
S1	123-45-6789	C2	7/21/03
S1	123-45-6789	C3	8/5/03
S1	123-45-6789	C4	8/5/03
S1	123-45-6789	C5	7/21/03
S2	234-56-7890	C2	7/25/03
S2	234-56-7890	C4	7/15/03
S3	345-67-8901	C3	8/1/03

This table represents the registrations for courses for students. It has the student ID, *sn*, the students social security number, *ssn*, the course registered for, and the date of the registration transaction. The FDs for this table are:

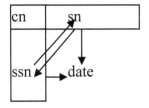

In this case the only non-key attribute is date, and it is clearly non-transitively FD on a candidate key. This table is 3NF. Notice the intra key FD's. There are two FDs that do not originate from a candidate key, *sn* → *ssn*, and *ssn* → *sn*. This table is not BCNF.

The update anomalies here are the same as the anomalies for tables that are only 1NF. Again, this table is doing two tasks. It is representing the registrations of students, and it is representing the student ID and social security number association. The table *Three* must be split into two tables. At this point it is important to distinguish between primary key and candidate key. The only way a table can be 3NF and not BCNF is for there to be multiple overlapping multiple attribute candidate keys. Only then can there be intra key FDs. When this table is split, the non-key attributes will go with one of the candidate keys, and the key attributes that are involved in the FDs will comprise the other table(s). The candidate key that goes with the non-key attributes should be the primary key. In this case the following SQL will generate the needed split.

CREATE TABLE Registrations AS   CREATE TABLE Students AS
SELECT DISTINCT sn, cn, date   SELECT DISTINCT sn, ssn
FROM Three;   FROM Three;

Registrations

sn	cn	street
S1	C1	7/21/03
S1	C2	7/21/03
S1	C3	8/5/03
S1	C4	8/5/03
S1	C5	7/21/03
S2	C2	7/25/03
S2	C4	7/15/03
S3	C3	8/1/03

Students

sn	ssn
S1	123-45-6789
S2	234-56-7890
S3	345-67-8901

Once again, the original table can be re-created by forming the *INNER JOIN* between these tables on *sn*.

This is not the only type of example of a table that is 3NF and not BCNF. It is easy to imagine a table where the non-key attribute is

FD on the candidate key, yet the non-key attribute determines an attribute in the key. Consider the case where there is a set of approved texts for each course. The teacher for a course may choose among the texts for their own section. The table *Text_Assignment* has three attributes, *Tn, Cn* and *Txn* where Txn is the unique identifier of a *Text*. For each *teacher course* pair there is exactly one *text* assigned. Therefore the pair (*Tn, Cn*) is the key for this table. The FDs for these attributes are as follows.

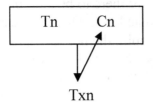

The table *Text_Assignment* is clearly 3NF and not BCNF. In order to make this table BCNF, it is split into two tables, (*Tn, Txn*) and (*Txn, Cn*). The information in the original *TextAssignment* table is recovered by the *INNER JOIN* of these tables.

If a table has only two attributes, then either one is FD on the other, or they determine each other. In either case, the table is BCNF. Every two-attribute table is BCNF.

Fourth Normal Form, 4NF

A table is 4NF if and only if it is BCNF and does not have any multi-valued dependencies.

Before 4NF can be defined it is necessary to define the concept of multi-valued dependency. This is a special kind of FD. These arise from the case that an attribute determines a multiple repeating groups. Consider the situation where a student may register for one or more courses, and may join one or more clubs. The following un-normalized table can be used to represent this.

Course-Club

Sn	Cn	Club
S1	C1 C2 C3 C4	 Chess Music
S2	C2 C4	Music Drama
S3	C3	Chess

Normalizing this table will yield the following 13 row table:

Course Club

Sn	Cn	Club
S1	C1	Chess
S1	C1	Music
S1	C2	Chess
S1	C2	Music
S1	C3	Chess
S1	C3	Music
S1	C4	Chess
S1	C4	Music
S2	C2	Music
S2	C2	Drama
S2	C4	Music
S2	C4	Drama
S3	C3	Chess

This table is clearly all key. Therefore, there is only one candidate key, and the table is clearly BCNF. Yet there are serious update anomalies. This is based on the fact that *Sn* determines two repeating groups. Each value of *Sn* determines a row with all combinations of the items in each of the repeating groups. This is what is known as a multi-valued dependency. In this case it is said that *Sn* multi-determines the pair *Cn* and *Club*. This is denoted as *Sn* -->> (*Cn, Club*).

If *S1* were to register for an additional course, *C5*, then two new rows would be required, (*S1, C5, Chess*), and (*S1, C5, Music*). However, if *S1* were to join the *Drama* club four new rows would be required, (*S1, C1, Drama*), (*S1, C2, Drama*), (*S1, C3, Drama*), and (*S1, C4, Drama*). On the other hand the addition of (*S4, C1, Music*) is the simple insertion of a single row. The update process is strongly dependant on the content of the table. This is clearly an unacceptable situation.

If each of the individual dependencies in the multi-valued dependency is split into a new table then these dependencies become simple FDs. Further, the INNER JOIN of these new tables will recreate the original set of combinations of the attribute values that were created when the multiple repeating group was normalized. None of these tables will have multi-valued dependencies, so they are 4NF.

CREATE TABLE Registrations AS
SELECT DISTINCT sn, cn
FROM Course_Club;

CREATE TABLE Clubs AS
SELECT DISTINCT sn, Club
FROM Course_Club;

Registrations

sn	cn
S1	C1
S1	C2
S1	C3
S1	C4
S2	C2
S2	C4
S3	C3

Students

sn	Club
S1	Chess
S1	Music
S2	Music
S2	Drama
S3	Chess

Tables that are not 4NF will be all key, or have a multiple attribute key that contains a multi-valued dependency. The multi-valued dependency will not be easy to spot by inspection of the values in a table. To detect 4NF problems, the table designer must be aware of multiple repeating groups among the attributes of the underlying business entity.

One more comment is in order about 4NF. If a table has only two columns, then it cannot contain a multi-valued dependency. Therefore, since it is automatically BCNF, it is also automatically 4NF.

Fifth Normal Form, 5NF

A table is in 5NF if and only if it is in 4NF, and every join dependency is a consequence of the candidate key. This normal form is often called the Projection-Join Normal Form, or PJNF.

A discussion of 5NF is included here for completeness sake. It will become clear that it will be very difficult to determine join dependencies. Further, it is difficult to imagine real cases where join dependencies exist. In all of the previous examples it has been possible to split the original table into two sets of attributes and recombine them using an *INNER JOIN* on the key columns to regain the original table. This is not always possible. There are cases (albeit rare) that the original table will only be recovered if the table is split into three or more tables that are *INNER JOINED*.

It is clear from the definition of 5NF that it is impossible, or at least impractical to detect if a table is 4NF but not 5NF. It would require extensive testing every time the contents of a table are changed. Further, this would be too late in the life cycle of the table to detect the problem. The table would already be populated, in use and have applications developed that use the table. It will be important to understand the types of situations where these tables can arise, and avoid these situations at design time.

Consider the following table. This table describes the media requirements of teachers for courses.

Schedules

Tn	Cn	Media
T1	C1	M2
T1	C2	M1
T2	C1	M1
T1	C1	M1

It is clear from inspection that this table is all key. Further, this table does not have any multi-valued dependencies. Since a teacher does not use all the same media types in all of the courses they teach, there are no repeating groups. This table is 4NF. Following are two projections of this table:

TC

Tn	Cn
T1	C1
T1	C2
T2	C1

CM

CN	Media
C1	M2
C2	M1
C1	M1

The INNER JOIN of these tables is:

TCM

Tn	Cn	Media
T1	C1	M2
T1	C1	M1
T1	C2	M1
T2	C1	M2
T2	C1	M1

There is a row that was not in the original table. Now form the *INNER JOIN* of this table with:

TM

Tn	Media
T1	M2
T1	M1
T2	M1

The result is the original table. This table is not 5NF.

The reason for this is that there is a complex business rule involving the three attributes that can only be represented by the *INNER JOIN* of the three tables. This rule states:

If Tx teaches Cy, and if Cy requires Mz, and if Tx uses Mz,
then it must be that Tx uses Mz in Cy.

This circular logic is clearly a very special business rule. It is not possible to model this business rule in a single table. This table must be split into all three tables, *TC, CM* and *TM*, and the *TCM* table must be represented as the *INNER JOIN* view that uses all three tables. If such a peculiar business rule exists, it should be discovered at design time for the database, and testing for *5NF* can be avoided.

Date[6] provides an excellent and complete discussion of *5NF*.

A Process for Producing Normalized Tables

Producing a set of normalized attributes from a collection of attributes is a part of the overall database design process that will be discussed more completely in the next chapter. The process basically involves four steps, removing join dependencies (if they can be found), removing multi-value dependencies, ensuring that all functional dependencies are determined by the primary key, and removing all repeating groups.

The following set of steps provide a useful process to normalization.

---

[6] An Introduction to Database Systems 6th ed., C. J. Date, Addison Wesley, 1997, ppxxxff.

- The first step is to gather the set of attributes that will be used to describe the instances of some entity. This will be the subject of much discussion in the next chapter. Among these attributes a unique identifier for the instances of the entity must be determined. This may, in fact, be a collection of the attributes.
- The next step is to remove all repeating groups of attributes by making separate instances of the entity for each repeated attribute. This will make the repeated attribute a part of the unique identifier.
- All of the functional dependencies among the attributes which are derived from business rules are determined. The transitive FDs are ignored. A set of tables are produced so that any attribute that determines another becomes the unique identifier in a table that contains all of the determined attributes.
- The next step is to remove all multi-value dependencies. These arise from the attribute set having multiple repeating groups. A table is formed for each of the repeated attributes. Each table has the unique identifier and one of the repeated attributes.
- Once the attributes have been determined circular logic business rules among groups of attributes are determined. These will be very rare. Each of the clauses in a circular logic business rule will generate a new business entity. Since these are so rare, no example will be presented.

It is important at this point to remember the reason tables are normalized. The object is to gain a design in which updates, insertions and deletes are not context sensitive. It may turn out that a functional dependency exists, however it is unlikely to cause update anomalies. It this functional dependency were to generate a new table, the database would be, in fact, more correct, but also somewhat more complex. If this gain in complexity does not remove likely update anomalies, then maybe the designer should ignore the functional dependency. A good designer will exercise good judgment in the normalization process.

To illustrate this process consider the following example. The entity being modeled is *Student*. A *Student* is characterized by the following attributes:

- Sn   student number
- Sname   the student name
- Street   the student permanent street address
- City   the student permanent city
- State   the student permanent state
- Zip   the student permanent zip
- Laddress   the residence hall address
- Lphone   the residence hall phone
- Major   the student major, (there may be more than one)
- Club   Student organization (there may be zero, one or many)

The unique identifier for a *Student* will be the *Sn*. These will be unique, and each student will have one. A school policy exists that the phone numbers for the residence hall rooms are actually fixed for the room. The FDs for this set of attributes can be graphically represented as follows.

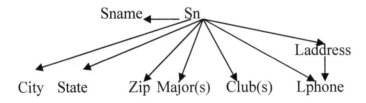

The first step is to eliminate the repeating groups. To do this, rows are repeated with the different values of each of the repeating groups. This makes the new unique identifier the attribute triple (*Sn, Major, Club*). The FDs for this entity now look like:

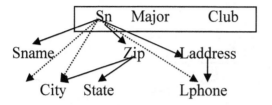

Now these attributes are placed in a set of BCNF tables by ensuring that any attribute that determines an FD becomes the unique identifier of an appropriately named table containing all of the determined attributes. The dashed FDs are transitive FDs, that is, they can be determined from a collection of other FDs. The transitive FDs are not used in producing BCNF tables. At this point some judgment must be exercised. The attribute *Zip* determines *City*, and *State*. This is because there is a relationship between these attribute values that is independent of the *Student* entity. The Postal Service maintains this relationship. At this point the designer must think about how important this relationship is. Questions the user must address are: What is the likelihood that an incorporation might occur which changes the *City* for a *Zip?*, What would the impact on the integrity of the data be?, What is the likelihood that data gathering and data entry errors will lead to inconsistencies in these attribute values?, and finally, What is the impact of inconsistencies in these values of the overall integrity of the data?. The answers can help the designer to decide whether to accept the additional complexity in design by creating a new entity with *Zip*, *City* and *State*, or to accept the risk of integrity problems and update anomalies by leaving the attributes in *Student*. In this case the relationships between *Zip* and Icity *and* between *Zip* and *State* are dropped. This makes the relationships between *Sn* and *City* and between *Sn* and *State* significant. On the other hand it is clear that the attribute pair *Laddress* and *Lphone* should be split off since the assignment of a phone number for a student is a direct consequence of the assignment of address.

The FDs that remain are:

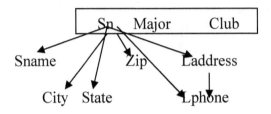

The new set of entities with the unique identifiers underlined is:

Students
Sn, Sname, Zip, City, State, Laddress

Room_Phones
Laddress, Lphone

Student_A
Sn, Major, Club

At this point all of the entities are BCNF. The designer will remember that there were two repeating groups in the original attribute set. Since a student may have multiple majors and may be in more than one club there are two repeating groups. This led to the multi-value dependency *Sn* -->>(*Major, Club*). The *Student_A* entity is not 4NF. It must be split into:

Student_Majors
<u>Sn</u>, Major

Student_Clubs
<u>Sn</u>, Club

These five entities are now 4NF.

In a discussion of these attributes with the Registrar, the Dean of Students and other business end-users, no circular logic traps were discovered among these attributes, so no join dependencies will exist. Therefore, these five entities are also 5NF.

9 ENTITY RELATIONSHIP MODELING

Introduction

The discussion in the previous chapter provided guidelines for the construction of entities from attribute sets that are well formed, and have no update anomalies. In this chapter the larger task is studied. This is the task of looking at the requirements of an enterprise system to determine what the entities are and how they are related to each other. This study is done in a very formal way yet embraces a natural conversation with the end-users. The objective is to design a precise and accurate database that embodies all of the business rules that pertain to the system at hand.

Entity-relationship modeling is a process that must involve business analysts and end-users. This is the process by which the requirements of a business system are described accurately for implementation in a database. For this reason, a good E-R modeling procedure will involve things for a DBA to do and things for a business analyst to do, and conversations that must occur between the two.

There are a number of different implementations of entity-relationship modeling, however they all produce the same results. The methods differ principally in their graphical representations.

The methodology that will be presented here is that used in the ORACLE Designer 2000® software. Richard Barker[7] provides an excellent text describing this process and some of the thought processes that will lead to a good model. David Hay[8] provides even more insight into the process. He looks at many of the business processes in a business and develops base-line E-R models for them. This methodology provides a graphical tool, a set of conversations that must occur with business analysts to ensure that the model is useful, and finally a database generation tool that actually produces a database that reflects the model designed. There is nothing that is done by the software that cannot be done easily by hand, so access to this software is not necessary for learning and implementing the methodology. All of the graphics and diagrams presented here were generated using the software, however it is easy to see that all of the work done here could easily be done with pencil and paper.

The first step is to understand what entities and their attributes are. This will draw upon the discussion of the previous chapter. Next will be a formal discussion of the ways in which entities can be related. This is a presentation of the relationships. This is followed by a discussion of how a precise database definition can be generated from the E-R diagram. This will be followed by examples that help the beginning designer develop some of the patterns of thinking that are needed to be successful at E-R diagramming.

Entities and Attributes

Entities are the material and conceptual objects in an enterprise about which data is stored. Entities are usually singular. The definition of an entity is the description of the nature of a business object. The collection of data that represents the actual instances of

---

[7] Richard Barker, <u>Case Methodology, Entity Relationship Modeling</u>, Addison Wesley Publishing, 1990.
[8] David C. Hay, <u>Data Model Patterns, Conventions of Thought</u>, Dorset House Publishing, New York, 1996.

the entity is stored in a database table derived from the entity. This process will be demonstrated later.

An entity is:

> *Any person, place, thing, event, thought, concept, or rule about which persistent data must be kept for the enterprise.*

Some obvious examples of entities are: *Student, Course, Teacher, Textbook* and *Classroom.* Some less clear entities might be, *Term,* the collection of dates over which a course is offered, *TextAssignment*, the specific text to be used in a course offering, and *Registration*, the event that links a student to a specific course offering. These entities appear to be used in some way to link other entities together in a meaningful way. The nature of these links will be discussed at length below.

Entities are described by their attributes. An attribute is a specific property of an entity. An attribute will have a specific data type, and will have a single well-defined value for each instance of an entity. Further, since missing values and *Null* values have serious consequences in the way they are handled, it is determined when an attribute is defined whether or not it will be allowed to have a *Null* value. For example, the *Student* entity might have attributes *sid* (an abbreviation for student ID), *name, age, religion, street, city, state, zip* (permanent address) *GPA, major1, major2, major3, club1, club2, club3,* etc. It is clear that the attributes must come from a discussion with the business analyst and the end-users. There will be many suggestions for attributes for each entity. Not all suggestions will become attributes. Some of the suggestions for descriptors for *Student* may have attributes of their own. For example *dormRoom*, is clearly a descriptor for *Student*, however, *dormRoom* will have attributes of its own such as *room#, building, size, capacity, cost,* etc. Since *DormRoom* has attributes of its own, it will become an entity. The fact that *DormRoom* is a descriptor of *Student* will be described in a relationship. This will be completely discussed below. Again, attributes will have a specific data type, and a specific well-defined value.

The alert reader will have noticed that the suggested entity *Student* is not very well defined. There are repeating groups, there are transitive functional dependencies among the attributes of *Student*, and there is a multi-valued dependency that arises from the multiple repeating groups. The definition of an entity must be normalized in exactly the same manner that was described for tables in the previous chapter. This will give rise to new entities such as *StudentPermAddress*, *StudentMajor* and *StudentClub*.

As in the case with relational tables, it must be possible to uniquely distinguish between all possible instances of an entity. This is done through the unique identifier for an entity. The unique identifier may be an attribute or set of attributes, or it may be that an entity is uniquely identified by the way in which it relates to other entities, or the unique identifier may be a combination of attributes and relationships. It is clear (from entity integrity) that any attribute that participates in the unique identifier must not be *Null*.

An entity is represented graphically by a round cornered rectangle. It contains the name of the entity, and a bulleted list of the attributes of the entity. Those attributes that participate in the unique identifier are denoted with # for bullets, those that may not accept *Null* values are denoted with solid bullets, •, and those that may accept *Null* values with open bullets, °.   For example:

Student: sid, name, age, religion picture goes here

Note that all of the other suggested attributes will appear in other entities that will somehow be related to *Student*.

When the Oracle Designer 2000 tool creates an entity the user is asked for the plural of the entity. This is because when a table is defined for the entity, the plural of the entity is used, and it is often the case that an acceptable plural cannot be generated by simply appending an 's' to the name of the entity. Additionally a *'Short Name'* is requested. This is because the entity name may be used in a combined way to name other objects such as foreign keys, linking entities, etc. The short name is used in these combinations.

Picture of the screen to create the student entity goes here.

The attributes of an entity are defined as a property of the entity. As an attribute is defined it is given a name, a data type or underlying domain, and the user decides whether or not the attribute may be optional. Additionally, to aid in the underlying table definition additional information can be provided such as the expected number of instances of an entity, and the expected growth rate for the entity. This information is stored in the Repository, and used when the tables are defined.

Picture of the screen for the properties of Student goes here.

Relationships

A relationship is defined simply as any significant association between two entities. The greatest variation between methodologies for notation in E-R modeling exists in the notation for relationships. Consider the entities *Student* and *StudentMajor.*

Remember that *StudentMajor* was generated to remove a repeating group. It contains an instance for each major that each student has chosen. If a student has chosen two majors, there will be two instances, if a student has a single major, there will be one instance, and if a student has not chosen a major, there will be no instances. A little thought will show that every instance of *Student* may be related to one or more instances of *StudentMajor*, while every instance of *StudentMajor* must be related to exactly one instance of *Student.* This relationship is described precisely by two sentences. Specifically,

Each *Student* may have one or more *StudentMajors*.

And

Each *StudentMajor* must be for one and only one *Student*.

Every relationship in an E-R model will relate two entities, and be described by two sentences. (This is not entirely true, but the exceptions will be clear later.) These sentences are of a very rigid and inflexible nature.

If *A* and *B* are two entities, then the relationship between *A* and *B* is described by two sentences:

	may		one or more			
Each	*A*	or	A-name	or	B	always
	must		one and only one			

	may		one or more			
Each	*B*	or	B-name	or	A	always
	must		one and only one			

where A-name and B-name are verbs that describe the relationship. In the case at hand,

Each *Student* may have one or more *StudentMajor*s always.

Each *StMajor* must be for one and only one *Student* always.

These sentences are represented graphically. The word *may* is represented by a broken line graphic at the end nearest the subject.

The word *must* is represented by a solid line graphic at the end nearest the subject. Since there are two sentences, and each of the entities appears as a subject in one, there will be a *may* or *must* (broken line or solid line) defined for each end of the relationship. In a similar manner, the phrase *one or more* will be represented by a fork (<) at the end nearest the object of the sentence, and the phrase *one and only one* will be represented by a straight line at the end of the relationship nearest the object of the sentence. Again, since there are two sentences, and each of the entities appears as the object of a sentence, there will be a graphic type for each entity. Finally each end of the relationship is named using the verb from the sentence for which the end is the object.

This may seem cumbersome and overly elaborate, but it is precise and complete. Further with just a small amount of practice it will become quite easy to draw relationships correctly, and to discern the underlying sentences from a diagram.

Each *Student* ma have one or more *StudentMajor*s always.

Each *StMajor* must be for one and only one *Student* always.

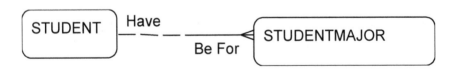

It is possible for an entity to be related to itself. That is, it is possible for some instances of an entity to satisfy some relationship with other instances. This is perfectly permissible. Consider the entity *Course*, and the prerequisite relationship. The first step is to write two sentences in the prescribed format that the business analyst and end user agree to. In this case:

Each *Course* may be prerequisite for one or more *Courses* always.

Each *Course* may have as prerequisite one or more *Courses* always.

Graphically:

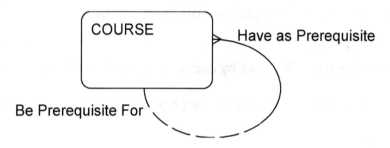

It is important at this point to discuss the difference between *may* and *must*. Consider the following diagram:

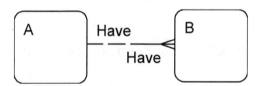

The associated sentences are:

Each *A* may have one or more *B* always.

Each *B* must have one and only one *A* always.

This means that in order for a *B* instance to <u>exist</u> it <u>must</u> be related to some instance of *A*. This is often interpreted incorrectly. The following example demonstrates nicely the fallacious thinking that leads to a common error. Consider the relationship between *Student* and *Course*. Intuitively, *Students* take *Courses* and *Courses* are taken by *Students*. It is possible to have a course that is never taken by a student. A common example would be a two credit-hour Independent Study course. These exist in many University Catalogs, yet are rarely used. Small projects earn one credit hour, and large projects earn three credit hours. On the other hand, the objective of a *Student* is to take *Courses* in order to earn a degree. One might be tempted to write these sentences:

Each *Course* may be taken by one or more *Students* always.

Each *Student* must take one or more *Courses* always.

This would indicate that a student could not exist until the student was taking a course! This would have a disastrous effect in the Admissions Office. It must be possible to have instances of *Students* that have not yet taken *Courses*. So, even though a *Student* must eventually take a *Course*, a *Student* can exist without having taken a *Course*. Correct versions of the sentences are:

Each *Course* may be taken by one or more *Students* always.

Each *Student* may take one or more *Courses* always.

And, the associated diagram is:

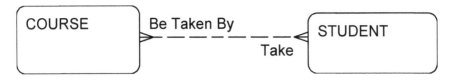

A relationship may participate in the definition of the unique identifier of an entity. For example, consider the entities *Author* and *Book*. It may not be reasonable to use the attribute *title* of *Book* as a unique identifier. There may be duplicate titles. However the *Author* that the *Book* is related to together with the *title* of the *Book* would make a reasonable unique identifier. This is signified by placing a hash mark on the relationship as shown in the diagram.

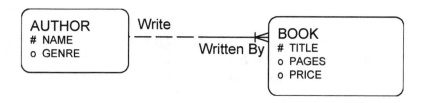

Sometimes there are cases when an instance of *B* was created for and associated with an instance of *A*. Further, this instance of *B* cannot be allowed to be re-associated with another instance of *A*. In this case the relationship from *A* to *B* is said to be non-transferable. For example, consider the relationships between *Course*, *CourseSection* and *Room*. When an instance if *CourseSection* is created it is created specifically for an instance of Course, so it should not be re-associated with another instance of *Course*. On the other hand when an instance of *CourseSection* is created it is associated with an instance of *Room*. It is completely reasonable to re-associate the *CourseSection* with another *Room*. Non-transferable relations are denoted by a diamond on the relationship as shown in the following diagram.

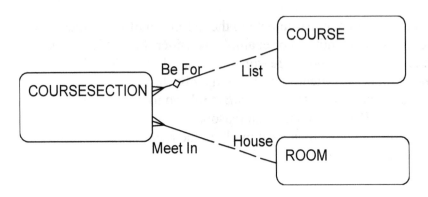

There are cases where an instance of *A* is related in the same way to either an instance of *B* or an instance of *C*. Consider the case of *ParkingPermit*, *Student*, and *Teacher*.

Each *Teacher* may be assigned one or more *ParkingPermits*.

Each *Student* may be assigned one or more *ParkingPermits*.

Each *ParkingPermit* is assigned to either one and only one *Teacher* or one and only one *Student*.

This is diagrammed as

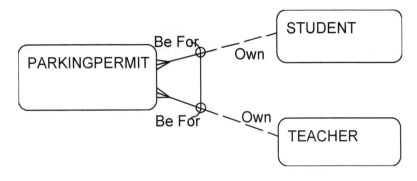

Valid Types of Relationships

Some of the types of relationships that can be drawn are more common than others, and in fact, some relationships that can be drawn cannot be physically manifested. Finally, while some can be drawn, and represent real situations, they are of little use without further analysis. The following discussion will present each type of relationship and for those that are legal, examples of where they might be useful.

Many-to-One Relationship Mandatory to Optional

This is the most common type of relationship. An example might be the relationship between a course offering (section) and a course.

Each *Section* must be of one and only one *Course* always.

Each *Course* may describe one or more *Sections* always.

In this case, a *Section* cannot exist unless it is for a specific *Course*, while there may be *Courses* with no *Sections*. The diagram is:

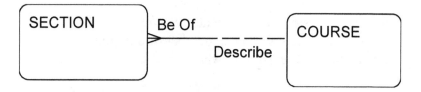

Many-to-One Relationship Mandatory to Mandatory

These are not common, but useful. They arise when the creation of one entity creates an associated set of instances of another entity. For example consider the case where a *Student Schedule* requires an advisor approval and the bursar approval. Further, the *Student Schedule* generates one or more *Registration* instances. A *Schedule* cannot exist without *Registrations*, and *Registrations* cannot exist without being for a *Schedule*.

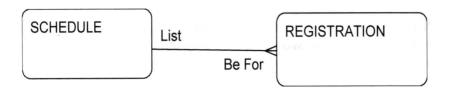

Many-to-One Relationship Optional to Mandatory

This relationship is equally uncommon. This is useful when exclusive groupings of instances of an entity are formed. For example, consider the case where *Students* may form project *Teams*. A *Student* will be a member of only one *Team*, if at all, and a Team will exist only when it is a group of *Students*.

Each *Team* must have one or more *Students* always.

Each *Student* may be on one and only one *Team* always.

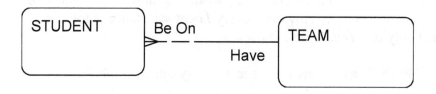

Many-to-One Relationship Optional to Optional

This relationship is used when both entities can exist without the other, yet there is an exclusive type constraint on membership. For example consider the case where a *Student's* GPA determines eligibility for an academic *Honorary*. An *Honorary* may or may not have *Student* members, and a *Student* may or may not join an *Honorary*, however a *Student* may join only one *Honorary*.

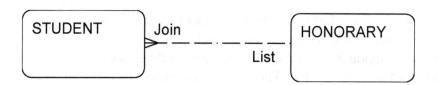

One-to-One Relationships Mandatory to Optional

This type of relationship is not common. It usually indicates a second entity which is in reality an optional set of attributes of the first entity. For example the case where there are full-time

Teachers and part-time *Teachers*. The full-time *Teachers* are all associated with a *Locator* instance. This has an office location, telephone, office hours, etc. The part-time *Teachers* may not have a *Locator* instance. However, every *Locator* instance is for one and only one *Teacher*.

Each *Teacher* may have one and only one *Locator Entry* always.

Each *Locator Entry* must be for one and only one *Teacher*.

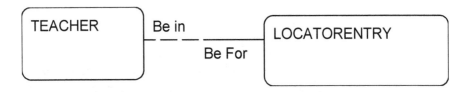

One-to-One Relationships Optional to Optional

● - - - - - - - - - - - - - -

This type of relationship often associates two different entities that may or may not be associated with each other, but when they are, the association is exclusive. For example, Libraries often have study carrels for faculty. These are places where faculty members may accumulate research materials for study. Many faculty are assigned to a carrel for research. There are also carrels that are not assigned. Of course, *Teachers* and *Carrels* can exist independently.

Each *Teacher* may be assigned to one and only one *Carrel*.

Each *Carrel* may be allocated to one and only one *Teacher*.

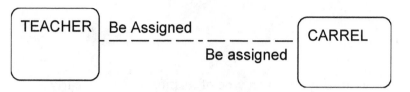

One-to-One Relationships Mandatory to Mandatory

● ———————————

This type of relationship links two entities that are actually two different views of the same entity. The two different views are maintained separately for clarity in understanding of a system. For example each *Student* will have a collection of demographic information such as address, permanent address, social security number, etc. Each *Student* will also have a collection of academic information such as GPA, hours completed, academic standing, etc. For simplicity of design it mat be clearer to create two entities, *StudentDemo*, and *StudentAcad*. These entities will be related as follows:

Each *StudentDemo* must be for one and only one *StudentAcad*.

Each *StudentAcad* must be for one and only one *StudentDemo*.

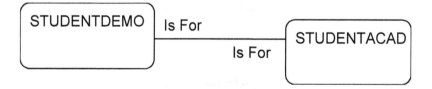

Many-to-Many Relationships Optional to Optional

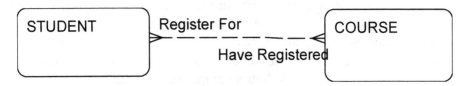

This is a reasonably common type of relationship in the early stages of model development. This relationship indicates that there is some as yet not specified entity that links the two entities. This entity is often conceptual in nature. For example consider the relationship between *Students* and *Courses*.

Each *Student* may register for one or more *Courses*.

Each *Course* may have registered one or more *Student*.

STUDENT	Register For — — — — —⟨ COURSE
	Have Registered

In this case there is the linking entity *Registration*.

Each *Student* may have one or more *Registrations*.

Each *Registration* must be for one and only one *Student*.

and,

Each *Course* may have one or more *Registrations*.

Each *Registration* must be for one and only one *Course*.

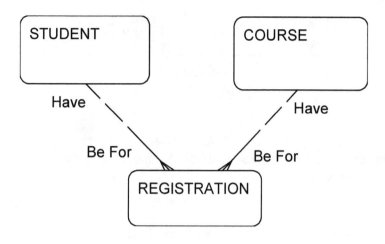

In this case the new entity *Registrations* links the entities *Students* and *Courses*. The name of the new entity is suggested by the names in the original many to many relationship.

It is always the case that such a linking entity exists. It is the responsibility of the designer to study the many-to-many relationship and determine the new linking entity and associated relationships. When these have been found, the original many-to-many relationship becomes redundant and should be removed from the diagram. Therefore, a completed diagram will have no remaining many-to-many relationships.

Consider in another example the relationship between *Courses* and *Books*.

Each *Course* may assign as text one or more *Books*.

Each *Book* may be assigned as text to one or more *Courses*.

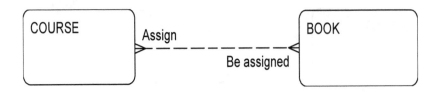

The new linking entity will have its name suggested by the clauses "assign as text" and "assigned as text to". In this the entity *TextAssignment* works well.

Each *Course* may have one or more *TextAssignments*.

Each *TextAssignment* must be for one and only one *Course*.

and,

Each *Book* may be in one or more *TextAssignments*.

Each *TextAssignment* must list one and only one *Course*.

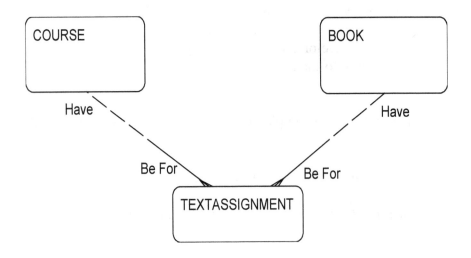

Note that the new linking entities often have no attributes. The unique identifier for the linking entity will be defined through its relationships to the linked entities. As described before, this is signified by a hash mark on the relationship.

Many-to-Many Relationships Mandatory to Optional

This relationship is very similar to the preceding relationship. It is used in cases where one of the entities cannot exist without at least one instance of the other. Consider the relationship between *StudyGroup* and *Student*. *Students* can be members of none, one or several *StudyGroups*, but *StudyGroups* do not exist unless they have members.

Each *Student* may belong to one or more *StudyGroups*.

Each *StudyGroup* must have one or more *Students*.

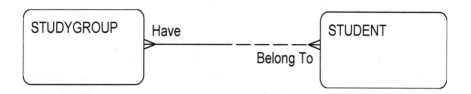

Like the previous relationship, this one must be studied further also. In this case there is a linking entity also. It is again suggested by the description of the relationship. For this case the entity *SGMembership* will work well.

Each *Student* may have one or more *SGMemberships*.

Each *SGMembership* must be for one and only one *Student.*

and,

Each *StudyGroup* must have one or more *SGMenberships*.

Each *SGMembership* must be for one and only one *StudyGroup.*

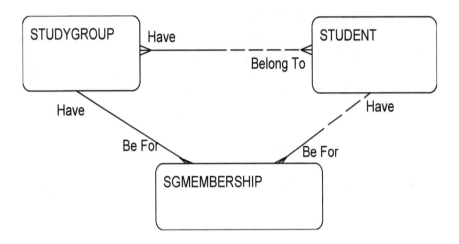

Note that the relationship between *Study Group* and *SGMembership* is "must" on both ends. This is the only difference in the way the many-to-many mandatory-to-optional relationship differs from the many-to-many optional-to-optional relationship.

Many-to-Many Relationships Mandatory to Mandatory

This relationship cannot exist. It indicates that no instance of either entity can exist without an associated instance of the other, yet the associations can be multiple. A little thought would lead the reader to see how this simply cannot happen.

Circular Relationships, Many to One

This type of relationship is used to create hierarchies. Consider the employment hierarchy,

Each *Person* may work for one and only one *Person*.

Each *Person* may manage one or more *Persons*.

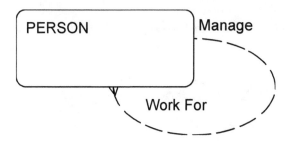

Note that neither end of this relationship can be mandatory, or infinite hierarchies are invented.

Circular Relationships, One to One

This relationship is used to indicate optional pairings between instances of an entity. A simple example is the marital relationship between instances of *Person*.

Each *Person* may be the mentor one and only one *Person*.

Each *Person* may be the mentee of one and only one *Person*.

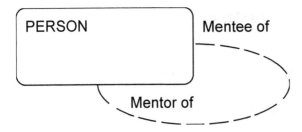

Circular Relationships, One to One, Mandatory to Mandatory

This relationship would be very unusual. It would indicate mandatory pairings between instances of an entity. Like in the previous example, mandatory pairings would be better represented by using another entity to represent the pairing.

An Example

The following example demonstrates some of the thought processes that are needed to develop a good entity relationship diagram for a business process. The example begins with a brief description of the business process. From this description it is possible to extract usable entities and their associated attributes and unique identifiers and relationships.

The Business Process Description

Classrooms are used for teaching course sections. Each section may be assigned to a classroom, or it may be left as TBA. This would be the case in a readings course that does not meet regularly. A classroom may be assigned to several sections. Each section has a single teacher of record. Before the rooms are assigned, each teacher will specify for each section a media-setup desired. The school has settled on four different media-setups. They are: "none", "projector and screen", "full presentation stack" and "teleconference". Each of the rooms has one of these four media-setups. Each of the pieces of equipment that has been installed in a room has an inventory number, a model number, a date purchased and a description. An application program will be written that matches the requirements of the faculty for each section with the classrooms.

The Entities

From the definition of an entity it is clear that all of the persons, places, things, events, etc that are relevant to this business process must be determined. Following is a list of nouns that might be candidates for entities.

classroom	course section	course
teacher	media-setup	piece of equipment
faculty	room	inventory number
description	model number	date purchased
none	projector and screen	full presentation stack
teleconference		

The first step is to eliminate candidates that are duplications or synonyms for other candidates. In this case *classroom* and *room* are clearly synonyms. Also *teacher* and *faculty* are synonyms. The next step is to eliminate all candidates that will likely be attributes of another entity since they will have no attributes themselves, and simply describe or relate to only one other entity. In this case, *inventory number, description, model number,* and *date purchased* all appear to be attributes of *piece of equipment*. All of those candidates should be eliminated. Finally all candidates that represent single instances of some other entity should be eliminated. Clearly *none, projector and screen, full presentation stack* and *teleconference* are instances of *media-setup*. These will be eliminated also. This leaves the following entity candidates.

classroom	course section	course
teacher	media-setup	piece of equipment

Next the entities are assigned singular clear descriptive names, all of the attributes of these entities are determined, whether or not the attribute is required and what its data type is determined for each entity in the list. This will usually require further discussion with the user community, and some intuition on the part of the designer. In this case the following will work. It is important to not include as attributes things that are themselves entities. This will be handled through the definition of relationships. The six remaining entities for this example are:

CLASSROOM	COURSE_SECTION	COURSE
• Bldg (string) • Room (string) • Capacity (integer)	• Section# (string) • Term (integer) •	• Number • Title • Description
TEACHER • Name (string)	MEDIA-SETUP • Type (string)	EQPT_ITEM • Inventory Number (string) ° Model Number (string) ° Date Purchased (date) • Description (memo)

The next step is to determine how these entities are related to each other. This is done by constructing pairs of sentences as above. If two entities relate to each other they will have a pair of sentences.

Classroom and Course_Section

A classroom may have several sections assigned to it. They will be at different times. On the other hand one of the local business rules is that a section is assigned to only one classroom if it even has one. Some sections have no classroom assignment. It seems clear that sections can exist independently of classrooms, and classrooms can exist independently of sections. With these facts in mind, the following two sentences can be constructed.

Each Section may be assigned to one and only one classroom.
Each Classroom may have assigned one or more sections.

The relationship is:

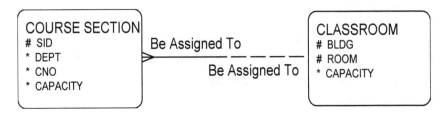

Course and Course Section

This is pretty clear. A section is an offering of a specific course. In the local business rules each section is for one particular course. A course can have several sections. It can also have no sections. A section cannot exist unless it is for a particular course, whereas courses can exist without sections. These facts lead to these sentences.

Each Course may have one or more sections.
Each Section must be of one and only one Course.

Adding this relationship, the diagram is:

156

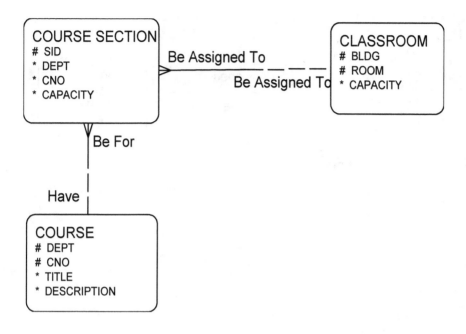

Course Section and Teacher

Sections have a teacher. In fact a local business rule states that there is only one teacher of record for each section. On the other hand teachers may have several sections. This is often the case. Experience indicates that sections can exist without teachers. Students notice this through the very busy teacher named Staff, or TBA that institutions publish in the course schedule information. Further, teachers can exist without sections. Occasionally a teacher is on leave or has an administrative assignment. These facts lead to these sentences.

Each section may be taught by one and only one teacher.

Each teacher may be assigned one or more sections.

The relationship is:

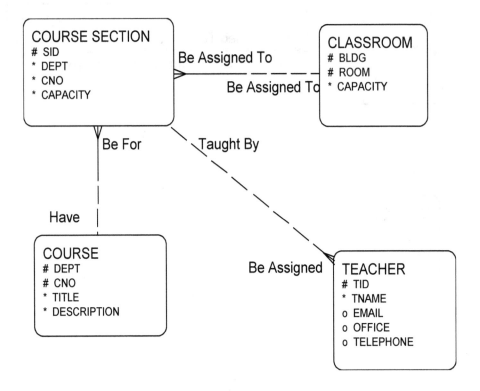

Teacher and Course

Teachers teach courses, and courses are taught by teachers. Further teachers may have favorite courses, and may even be famous for certain courses. The only relationship between teachers and courses that is germane in the context of room scheduling, however is the relationship that is described transitively through course section. Therefore there is no new relationship here. Not every pair of entities has a relationship, and for those pairs that do have relationships, not all relationships are germane to the description of the process. The designer must ferret all of this out through discussion with the end users.

Converting An ER Diagram to a Database

Once an entity relationship diagram is complete, it is a relatively simple task to generate a database that supports all of the business rules embodied in the diagram. All of the judgment and decision-making has been accomplished in the development of the entity relationship diagram. The process of generating a database is so automatic that it can be programmed. This is a part of the ORACLE Designer 2000 system. The use of this system will be demonstrated later.

The basic algorithm is:

- Create a table for each entity. Make the table name be the plural of the entity name. Make each attribute of the entity a column in the table with the appropriate data type. Make the primary key of the table be the unique identifier of the entity. This may require adding columns that are attributes from other relations. To name these columns use the concatenation of the short names for the entities and the short names for the attributes. This may be an iterative process. That is, if entity *A* receives its unique identifier from entity *B*, and entity *B* in turn receives its unique identifier from entity *C*, then table B must be created first, the table A.

- For each many-to-one relationship place new columns in the table representing the entity at the "many" end for all of the attributes of the unique identifier of the entity at the "one" end. These new columns will be named using the concatenation of the short names for the entities and the short names for the attributes. The columns will be allowed to accept NULL if the many relationship is optional, otherwise they will be restricted *NOT* NULL. These new columns will become a foreign key on the table at the other end.

- Each one-to one relationship place new columns in the tables representing both ends. The new columns in the table representing one end are the attributes representing the unique identifier of the entity at the other end. The columns are allowed to accept *NULL* if the relationship is optional at this end, otherwise the columns are restricted to be *NOT NULL*. These new columns will become a foreign key on the table at the other end. The other end is treated exactly the same way. In short, the tables at each end receive new columns from the other end as foreign keys.

- Any many-to many relationships that remain, (in a good design there will be none) will lead to new tables that are not based on an entity. These are linking tables. A new table is created whose name is the concatenation of the short names of the entities at each end of the relationship. All of the attributes that form the unique identifiers of both entities are added as columns of the new table. All of the columns of the new table become the primary key. There will be two foreign keys. All of the columns that came from the entity at one end will become a foreign key on the table representing the entity. The other attributes will become a foreign key in the table representing the entity at the other end.

There are other steps in this process for handling exclusive or relationships, and nested entities. These will be skipped here. This all sounds very daunting until it is applied to an example. Consider the following se of entities and relationships. They describe the registrations of students in course sections, and the assignment of students to mentors. The business rule here is that a student may have a student mentor, and a student may be mentor of one or more students. The mentoring relationship represents a recursive relationship. These model the same, however since a table will gain a foreign key on itself, the concept is often confusing. Therefore, this will be an important example to study. The entity relationship diagram is:

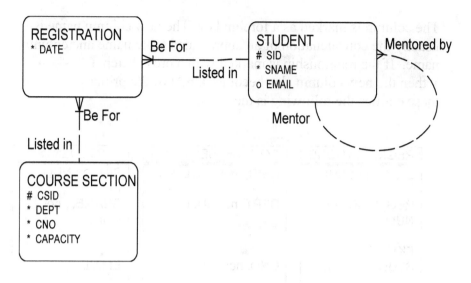

The first step of the algorithm would generate three tables, one for each entity. The tables would be REGISTRATIONS, COURSE_SECTIONS and STUDENTS.

The attributes from the entities would become columns of the tables. Required attributes become not NULL columns. Those columns that are marked as part of the unique identifier become part of the primary key.

REGISTRATIONS	COURSE_SECTIONS	STUDENTS
DATE, not NULL	CSID, not NULL PK	SID, not NULL PK
	DEPT, not NULL	SNAME, not NULL
	CNO, not NULL	EMAIL
	CAPACITY, not NULL	

The next step is to insert those columns that would become foreign keys. Each many-to-one attribute will gain a column in the table at the many end which is the primary key of the table at the one end.

The column is marked as a foreign key. The new column name is usually the concatenation of an abbreviated table name and column name. If the relationship is marked with a cross hatch, (>-|--------), then the new column also becomes a part of the primary key. For these entities the following is the result.

REGISTRATIONS	COURSE_SECTIONS	STUDENTS
DATE, not NULL	CSID, not NULL PK	SID, not NULL PK
REG_CSID not NULL, (PK, FK)	DEPT, not NULL	SNAME, not NULL
STUD_SID not NULL, (PK, FK)	CNO, not NULL	EMAIL
	CAPACITY, not NULL	STUD_MENTOR, FK

It is now easy to generate SQL to construct the tables and key constraints.

```
CREATE TABLE COURSE_SECTIONS
(CAPACITY INTEGER NOT NULL,
DEPT VARCHAR(240) NOT NULL,
CNO VARCHAR(240) NOT NULL,
CSID VARCHAR(240) NOT NULL) ;

CREATE TABLE REGISTRATIONS
(REG_DATE VARCHAR(240) NOT NULL,
CSEC_CSID VARCHAR(240) NOT NULL,
STUD_SID VARCHAR(240) NOT NULL) ;

CREATE TABLE STUDENTS
(SID VARCHAR(240) NOT NULL,
EMAIL VARCHAR(240),
SNAME VARCHAR(240) NOT NULL,
```

STUD_SID VARCHAR(240)) ;

ALTER TABLE COURSE_SECTIONS
ADD CONSTRAINT CSEC_PK PRIMARY KEY(CSID);

ALTER TABLE REGISTRATIONS
ADD CONSTRAINT REG_PK PRIMARY
KEY(CSEC_CSID,STUD_SID);

ALTER TABLE STUDENTS
ADD CONSTRAINT STUD_PK PRIMARY KEY(SID);

ALTER TABLE REGISTRATIONS
ADD CONSTRAINT REG_STUD_FK FOREIGN KEY
(STUD_SID)
        REFERENCES STUDENTS(SID);

ALTER TABLE REGISTRATIONS
ADD CONSTRAINT REG_CSEC_FK FOREIGN KEY
(CSEC_CSID)
        REFERENCES COURSE_SECTIONS(CSID);

ALTER TABLE STUDENTS
ADD CONSTRAINT STUD_STUD_FK FOREIGN KEY
(STUD_SID)
        REFERENCES STUDENTS(SID);

Key Words:

ABSOLUTE
ACTION
ACTOR
ADD
AFTER
ALIAS
ALLOCATE
ALTER
ARE
ASSERTION
ASYNC
AT
ATTRIBUTES
BEFORE
BETWEEN
BIT
BIT_LENGTH
BOOLEAN
BOTH
BREADTH
CALL
CASCADE
CASCADED
CASE
CAST
CATALOG
CHAR_LENGTH
CHARACTER_LEN
GTH
COALESCE
COLLATE
COLLATION
COLUMN
COMPLETION
CONNECT
CONNECTION
CONSTRAINT

CONSTRAINTS
CONVERT
CORRESPONDING
CROSS
CURRENT_DATE
CURRENT_PATH
CURRENT_TIME
CURRENT_TIMES
TAMP
CURRENT_USER
CYCLE
DATA
DATE
DAY
DEALLOCATE
DEFERRABLE
DEFERRED
DEPTH
DEPTH
DESCRIBE
DESCRIPTOR
DESTROY
DIAGNOSTICS
DICTIONARY
DISCONNECT
DO
DOMAIN
DROP
EACH
ELEMENT
ELSE
ELSEIF
ELSEIF
END-EXEC
EQUALS
EXCEPT
EXCEPTION
EXECUTE
EXTERNAL
EXTRACT

FACTOR
FALSE
FIRST
FULL
GENERAL
GET
GLOBAL
HOLD
HOUR
IDENTITY
IF
IGNORE
IMMEDIATE
INITIALLY
INNER
INPUT
INSENSITIVE
INSTEAD
INTERSECT
INTERVAL
ISOLATION
JOIN
LAST
LEADING
LEAVE
LEAVE
LEFT
LESS
LEVEL
LIMIT
LIST
LOCAL
LOOP
LOWER
MATCH
MINUTE
MODIFY
MONTH
NAMES
NATIONAL

NATURAL	RIGHT	UPPER
NCHAR	ROLE	USAGE
NEW	ROUTINE	USING
NEW_TABLE	ROW	VALUE
NEXT	ROWS	VARCHAR
NO	SAVEPOINT	VARIABLE
NONE	SCROLL	VARYING
NULLIF	SEARCH	VIRTUAL
OBJECT	SECOND	VIRTUAL
OCTET_LENGTH	SENSITIVE	VISIBLE
OFF	SEQUENCE	WAIT
OID	SESSION	WHEN
OLD	SESSION_USER	WHILE
OLD_TABLE	SIGNAL	WHILE
ONLY	SIMILAR	WITHOUT
OPERATION	SIZE	WRITE
OPERATOR	SPACE	YEAR
OPERATORS	SQLEXCEPTION	ZONE
OTHERS	SQLSTATE	
OUTER	SQLWARNING	
OUTPUT	START	
OVERLAPS	STATE	
PAD	STRUCTURE	
PARAMETERS	SUBSTRING	
PARTIAL	SYMBOL	
PATH	SYSTEM_USER	
PENDANT	TEMPORARY	
POSITION	TERM	
POSTFIX	TEST	
PREFIX	THEN	
PREORDER	THERE	
PREPARE	TIME	
PRESERVE	TIMESTAMP	
PRIOR	TIMEZONE_HOUR	
PRIVATE	TIMEZONE_MINU	
PROTECTED	TE	
READ	TRAILING	
RECURSIVE	TRANSACTION	
REF	TRANSLATE	
REFERENCING	TRANSLATION	
RELATIVE	TRIGGER	
REPLACE	TRIM	
RESIGNAL	TRUE	
RESTRICT	TUPLE	
RETURN	TYPE	
RETURNS	UNDER	
REVOKE	UNKNOWN	

ABOUT THE AUTHOR

John Starner is an Associate Professor of Mathematics and Computer Science at St. Thomas University in Houston.